Complex Predicates and Information Spreading in LFG

STANFORD MONOGRAPHS IN LINGUISTICS

The aim of this series is to make exploratory work
that employs new linguistic data, extending the scope or domain
of current theoretical proposals, available to a wide audience.
These monographs will provide an insightful generalization of the
problem and data in question which will be of
interest to people working in a variety of frameworks.

STANFORD MONOGRAPHS IN LINGUISTICS

COMPLEX PREDICATES AND INFORMATION SPREADING IN LFG

Avery D. Andrews
&
Christopher D. Manning

CSLI
PUBLICATIONS
Center for the Study of
Language and Information
Stanford, California

Copyright © 1999
CSLI Publications
Center for the Study of Language and Information
Leland Stanford Junior University
Printed in the United States
03 02 01 00 99   5 4 3 2 1

Library of Congress Cataloging-in-Publication Data

Andrews, Avery D. (Avery Delano), 1949–
Complex predicates and information spreading in LFG / Avery D. Andrews,
Christopher D. Manning.
p.   cm.
Includes bibliographical references (p.) and index.
ISBN 1-57586-165-8 (alk. paper).
ISBN 1-57586-164-X (pbk. : alk. paper)

1. Lexical-functional grammar. 2. Grammar, Comparative and general–Verb
phrase. I. Manning, Christopher D. II. Title.
P158.25.A53   1999
415—dc21   98-45541
CIP

"Constructions des Lisse", the drawing on the cover of the paperback edition of
this book, is from *Encyclopédie ou Dictionnaire Raisonné des Sciences des Arts
et des Métiers*, edited by Diderot. Première Édition de 1751–1780.

∞ The acid-free paper used in this book meets the minimum requirements of
the American National Standard for Information Sciences—Permanence of
Paper for Printed Library Materials, ANSI Z39.48-1984.

CSLI was founded early in 1983 by researchers from Stanford University, SRI
International, and Xerox PARC to further research and development of integrated
theories of language, information, and computation. CSLI headquarters and CSLI
Publications are located on the campus of Stanford University.

CSLI Publications reports new developments in the study of language, information,
and computation. In addition to monographs, our publications include lecture notes,
working papers, revised dissertations, and conference proceedings. Our aim is to make
new results, ideas, and approaches available as quickly as possible. Please visit our web
site at
http://csli-publications.stanford.edu/
for comments on this and other titles, as well as for changes and corrections by the
author and publisher.

Contents

Preface

This work began out of some discussions, email, and short papers exchanged between the authors in the late eighties. Andrews had noted certain constructions, such as scoping modifiers, which created problems for LFG, whereas GPSG and HPSG seemed to handle them with aplomb. He had observed that an idea of Manning's, whereby f-structure construction was viewed as the formation of equivalence classes, might help, and had suggested to Manning that he look at Romance complex predicates, which Manning then did. It then seemed that if these two topics were put together the result might look like something. The outcome was Andrews and Manning (1993).

The present monograph applies the basic ideas and themes of this earlier work to the analysis of various kinds of complex predicates, including a few types of 'serial verbs'. Although the underlying ideas are those of the earlier work, there are some significant technical differences. Andrews and Manning (1993) relied on what might be called 'headship relations', such as a grammatical function H which the head of an X-bar phrase would bear to its mother, in a manner similar to HPSG. There were then principles formulated as 'constructive conditionals' which would have the effect of enforcing sharing of the values of certain attributes, such as morphosyntactic features, across the H-relation. Different headship relations enforced spreading of different classes of attributes, allowing various kinds of information spreading effects to be produced by appropriate deployment of the headship relations.

Although we retain the idea of having a flexible implementation of different patterns of spreading for different classes of attributes, we have replaced the use of headship relationships with the use of a kind of restriction. There are two main motivations for this, one essentially theoretical, the other empirical. The empirical motivation is that the variety of spreading patterns that are found seems to be rather larger than we had imagined in 1993. Then we seemed to need only a few labels to control the spreading of several different classes of features in combination, whereas it seems better now to control each class individually, as may be easily achieved via the notion of 'positive restriction' that we introduce in Chapter 1. The theoretical motivation is to make a clearer, simpler, and more constrained addition to the formal ontology of LFG. Our notion of positive restriction is a modest addition to LFG, if it is an addition at all, because it is a basic set-theoretical concept already used in the definition of 'negative restriction' in Kaplan and Wedekind (1993). The use of 'constructive conditionals' in the 1993 version was by itself unproblematic, since, as we showed, they can be interpreted merely as a convenient syntactic shorthand for expressing relations that were already available in the LFG description logic. However, the mechanism for feature spreading then involved the introduction of headship attributes and statements expressed as universal quantification over constructive conditionals. The headship attributes were a somewhat messy addition, and the quantified statements required going beyond the bounds of the quantifier-free logic of identity that has by and large been sufficient for other LFG analyses. Although the work of Johnson (1991) shows that the required kinds of statements (which fall into the Schönfinkel-Bernays class, as discussed in Andrews and Manning (1993)) could be added to the LFG formalism without destroying decidability, the computational consequences could still be unpleasant.

In contrast, the present restrictions approach involves an appealingly simple modification to the formal framework, and should not involve any deterioration in computational performance. LFG has had a vision of multiple parallel levels of representation, related by correspondence functions, but as we show in Appendix B, the use of a 'projection architecture' (Kaplan 1995) to implement this has technical problems. Here we offer a slightly different picture of multiple kinds of information which differ not in the level on which they are put, but by how they spread. As we show, this allows the maintenance of traditional LFG analyses, while fixing technical problems and opening up new avenues for the analysis of new empirical data. The notion of positive restrictions is offered as a general formal device, and we hope the reader can gain some flavor of that from the brief discussions of X-bar theory and scoping modifiers in Chapter 1.

A second change from Andrews and Manning (1993) is the introduction of hierarchical argument-lists, first introduced in HPSG, and applied to the cross-linguistic typology of grammatical relations by Manning (1996a). While it would be possible to formulate complex-predicate formation operations without such lists, we believe that their use helps constrain the possibilities, and strengthens the connections between the theory of grammatical relations and the theory of complex-predicate formation.

While the implications of the proposals made here are quite far-reaching, the recent interests of the authors have meant that the majority of this monograph is about complex predicates, and in particular, serial verbs. Our study of serial verbs significantly expands the range of data that has been treated under the 'complex predicate' label in LFG, but nevertheless, has in the main left us with a sense of how much further typological research into different construction types in different languages is needed, and this will hopefully be a topic for further research.

Acknowledgments

We have had many kinds of assistance from different groups of people in the preparation of this work. Audiences at the Stanford linguistics department, Xerox PARC, and LFG conferences listened to presentations and made pertinent suggestions, and we have benefitted from discussions with Ron Kaplan, John Maxwell, Mary Dalrymple and especially Joan Bresnan. We have also received a great deal of help with examples and discussion of particular language analyses from Alexandra Aikhenvald, Maria Bittner, and Ken Hale, and very helpful comments on preliminary versions of the ms. from Miriam Butt, Jane Simpson, and Stephen Wilson.

We thank our current institutions, the Australian National University, and the the University of Sydney for supporting this research. And finally we would like to thank the institutions, faculty and support staff at CSLI, Stanford Linguistics and Xerox PARC for making our lives easier and more pleasant than they might have been, for Chris Manning as a student and Avery Andrews as an occasional visitor; Avery Andrews would especially like to thank Joan Bresnan for sponsoring visits, and Jeanette Figueroa for feats such as pre-organizing accomodation even though there basically wasn't any available.

1

Introduction

A central idea in most of the grammatical theories that have been developed over the the last thirty years has been a notion of 'head', not always very well defined, but often understandable in terms of information-sharing or dependency. For example, in a simple French noun phrase such as (1), the noun might be regarded as the head because it determines the feminine gender-feature, which is then shared (or inherited by), the entire noun-phrase:

(1)

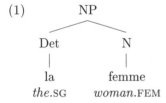

The explication of headship in terms of information-sharing has been particularly exploited in Lexical-Functional Grammar (Bresnan 1982), where simple sharing of information between mother and daughter nodes plays a crucial role in the analysis of most grammatical phenomena. Not only is such feature sharing used to account for properties such as case, agreement, and tense, but, for example, the valence properties of a predicate and the grammatical relations it subcategorizes are shared between the head and mother nodes. This contrasts with frameworks such as Head-driven Phrase Structure Grammar (Pollard and Sag 1994), Categorial Grammar (Morrill 1994), or Construction Grammar (Goldberg 1995, Fillmore and Kay in prep), where the valence of the mother is derived from the valence of the head via a process of argument cancellation.

But in spite of the centrality of this device, only one form of mother-daughter information-sharing is explicitly investigated in most of the major LFG analyses, namely, sharing of f-structures. In contrast, this work argues for the recognition of a number of forms of differential information spreading, and presents a reformulation of LFG that better supports such a conception of grammar, in which headship, understood in terms of information-sharing, is inherently multidimensional rather than unitary.

There are various uses for this new flexibility, and several of them are touched on in this chapter. For example the headship relations in (1) are in fact controversial: although it is traditional to regard the noun as head, a case can be made that the head is in fact the determiner.[1] With a multidimensional concept of headship based on information-spreading, we can analyse (1) as having both the Det and N as co-heads for many purposes (under standard LFG analyses, they have the same f-structure), while still allowing one or the other to serve as head in terms of other properties, should this be required.

However, the main empirical domain dealt with in this monograph is one that has been important in much recent work: the analysis of 'complex predicates', defined in (Alsina et al. 1997:1) as predicates that are multi-headed, in the sense that "they are composed of more than one grammatical element (either morphemes or words) each of which contributes part of the information ordinarily associated with a head." Complex predicates so-defined include the light verb and many of the serial verb constructions found in various languages. Consider as an example the following serial verb complex predicate from Tariana (Aikhenvald to appear b) – a construction discussed in detail in Chapter 4:

(2) naː-na   dura   du-pita   du-yã-nhi
    3PL-ACC 3SGF.order 3SGF-bathe 3SGF-stay-IMPF
    'She ordered them to bathe.'

In this sentence there are three verbs, the second and third of which have a different actor (or logical subject) from the first, though all of them agree with the person doing the ordering. As we argue more extensively later, the correct analysis appears to be that this sentence should be regarded as a single clause. Such constructions: (i) show distinctive concordant agreement with a single subject, (ii) have the intonational properties of a single clause, not of a coordination or sequence of clauses, (iii) do not contain the markers of syntactic dependency found in clear cases of subordinate and coordinate clauses, and (iv) provide a single domain for the expression of markers of tense, aspect, modality, and polarity, as is so commonly found in serial verb constructions (Durie 1997). However, implementing such an analysis is difficult in 'Classic LFG' (the theory and approach of Bresnan (1982)), because it was really only designed to handle clauses that contained a single argument taking predicate. To be able to represent both all the sharing that goes on (such as the sharing of tense, aspect, and modal-

---

[1]See for example (Hudson 1990:271), who mentions (Lyons 1977:464) and others as early sources. In generative grammar, the arguments and analyses of (Abney 1987) have been particularly influential for the rather wide acceptance of this kind of analysis.

ity throughout the clause) and the distinctions (the verbs have different meanings and the first verb is the semantic head which takes the remaining verbs as some sort of semantic argument), we need to introduce more flexible concepts of headship and information spreading. In order to show this, we will briefly present the architecture of Classic LFG and then some of the arguments for extending it.

F-structures in LFG are complex feature structures which combine information about grammatical relations (used to drive semantic composition of the meanings of predicates with those of their arguments), grammatical features (used to account for phenomena of morphological government and concord), and the lexical semantics and valences of the heads of phrases (encoded in the value of the PRED-feature). LFG structures sentences by giving them a surface phrase-structure tree called a c-structure, each of whose nodes corresponds to an f-structure, through a correspondence function ϕ. Here, for example, are the c- and f-structures for a simple sentence, with the correspondence between them represented by the arrows:

(3)

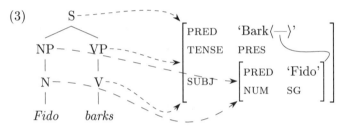

Observe that the S, VP and V all correspond to a single f-structure, which is the f-structure of the whole sentence, and the NP and N correspond to another, which is the value of SUBJ within the full structure. Because of this sharing of f-structures, lexical properties of the N *Fido*, such as being singular, become properties of the NP that *Fido* is head of, and likewise properties of the verb *barks*, such as being present tense, intransitive, and taking a third person singular subject, become properties of the dominating VP and S nodes, implementing mother-daughter information sharing. These sharing patterns motivating calling N the head of NP, V the head of VP, and VP the head of S.

In Classic LFG, the content of the f-structures and the correspondence connecting its parts to the c-structure nodes are specified by local principles that are formulated as annotations to phrase-structure rules. These annotations state properties and relations between the correspondents of a node and its mother in terms of the arrow symbols ↑, referring to the f-structure correspondent of the mother, and ↓, referring to the f-structure correspondent of the node the annotation appears on. Hence a rule such as:

(4) S → NP VP
  (↑ SUBJ) = ↓ ↑ = ↓

says that the f-structure correspondent of the daughter NP should be the SUBJ-value of the f-structure correspondent of the S, and the f-structure correspondent of the daughter VP should be the same as that of the S (rendering VP the head of S, in terms of f-structural properties). Annotations are required to satisfy certain principles, such as Functional Locality, which are part of the substantive linguistic theory of LFG, and f-structures are required to satisfy certain conditions, such as Completeness and Coherence, for the sentence to be deemed well-formed. See Kaplan and Bresnan (1982) and Kaplan (1995) for a formal account of the notation and structure of the theory.

More recent linguistic work within LFG (Alsina 1996, Bresnan in prep) has sought to replace such stipulated equations on phrase structure rules with general and universal principles which effect the same sharing relationships and assignment of grammatical functions. While such an approach has greater explanatory potential, and is to be preferred to the more stipulative equations of early LFG, the result is the same kind of feature sharing, and so we will present our account within the traditional conception, in order to keep the focus on our specific innovations.

Applying similar annotations or principles to the NP and VP rules, together with lexical entries, produces an annotated tree such as the one in (5) (note that the annotations have been placed above the items they appear on, so that the arrows point to what they refer to):

(5)

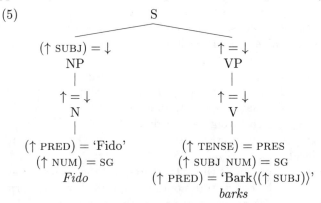

These annotations constitute a collection of assertions that can be solved to yield the full linguistic structure (3), as discussed in Kaplan and Bresnan (1982).

A good way to illustrate the effect of the $\uparrow = \downarrow$ annotations is to draw loops around the sets of nodes that are connected by these annotations, and then to connect the loops to the f-structures:

(6)

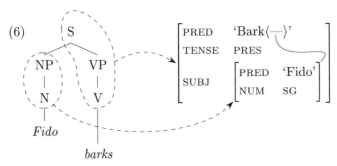

The combination of attribute-sharing between mothers and daughters, and unification[2] of the values of attributes that are thereby equated provides the basis for a great deal of appropriate descriptive power at an extremely modest formal cost.

However, in spite of the considerable utility of f-structure sharing between mothers and their daughters, there are a variety of phenomena that show that it is not flexible enough, and does not provide a sufficiently general concept of headship. A large body of work in various theoretical frameworks, including earlier work in LFG has argued for a framework that allows multiple notions of headship.[3] In the remainder of this section we will sketch a few cases where more complicated feature sharing relationships are motivated. We will then outline an architecture which supports differential feature sharing, that is, multidimensional headship, in a more flexible and empirically adequate manner than has been previously available in LFG.

1 Arguments for multiple notions of head and differential spreading

A very simple case is the X-bar theory of phrase structure. The basic idea of X-bar theory is that the inventory of phrasal categories in a language can be generated from its lexical categories, via a system of diacritic features (realized perhaps as a 'BAR' feature) that distinguish various phrasal levels, such as the lexical category itself ('BAR 0') and its maximal phrase (these days normally taken as 'BAR 2'). The lexical category and level-diacritic

---

[2]There are various technical concepts of unification available, but we take the essence of the idea to be 'and' in a logic or descriptive system where consistency is decidable, so that contradictory information can be detected by an algorithm.

[3]E.g., Simpson (1983), Ackerman and LeSourd (1997:86), and Corbett et al. (1993), especially the paper by Zwicky and Corbett.

features cross-classify the phrase-types, so that an NP or VP will agree in lexical category but not level-diacritic with its N or V head.

This sharing of lexical category information seems quite similar to the sharing of f-structure information, and one might think to put the category information into the f-structure, but there are various reasons why this does not work out. An exceptionally clear instance is Alsina's (1996:150–160) demonstration that 'indirect objects' in Romance languages behave as direct arguments, and thus have simple f-structures just like plain NPs, even though they have the c-structures of PPs. Here for example is the structure of a Spanish indirect object PP such as **a los niños** 'the children':

(7)

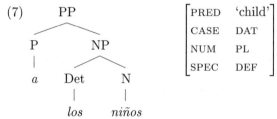

Alsina shows that we want the entire PP and NP together to correspond to a single f-structure, while, for the c-structure, we want the P and PP to share their lexical category, and also the N and NP; but we do not want to share the lexical category between the NP and the PP.[4] It appears that the lexical category features spread in a manner similar to f-structure features, but somewhat less aggressively. And of course the diacritic features will share less aggressively still; in fact hardly at all in some versions of X-bar theory, such as that of Jackendoff (1977).

More complex examples from X-bar theory are provided by Kroeger (1993) and Bresnan (in prep), who analyse clause-level phrase-structure in terms of a combination of 'extended projections' of the VP (phrases such as IP and CP that share the f-structure with the VP but differ in at least some category features), and an exocentric category 'S' which again shares an f-structure with a VP or other phrase underneath it, but does not share its category. For instance, one might propose a structure as in (8) for a sentence in the VSO language Welsh. Again, we wish to share f-structure information throughout the extended projection that encompasses the V, VP, S, I and IP nodes (shown in bold in (8); ↑ = ↓ annotations omitted), but not category information, which should be shared only between $\overline{\text{X}}$-

---

[4]The status of the Det is unclear: if we accept the DP hypothesis (Abney 1987), we would want to rearrange the tree so that the Det was an X-bar head taking an NP as its complement, so there would be a third lexical category to spread; under the more traditional structure presented here, Det might be a nominal category with some additional diacritic.

heads and their mothers (I and IP on the one hand, and V and VP on the other):

(8)

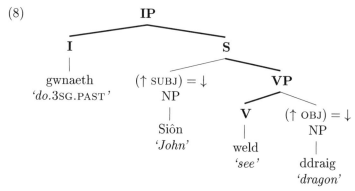

Another difficulty with f-structure sharing is when the identifications at f-structure result in too much feature sharing for other purposes, such as for semantic interpretation. As we have observed, the f-structure tends to flatten the phrase structure by implementing sharing between nodes. This is problematic if the flatter f-structure is no longer sufficient to guide semantic interpretation of the sentence. A case where it makes serious trouble is in the interpretation of 'concentrically scoped' modifiers (Andrews 1983):

(9) An alleged former racketeer was elected.

In most unification-based theories, these examples are completely unproblematical (see, for instance, Pollard and Sag 1994, Ch. 8). But the standard use of level-flattening and sets to represent adjuncts creates severe difficulties for LFG. The prenominal adjectives are standardly treated as members of a set-valued ADJUNCT GF, producing an f-structure such as this for (9):

(10)
$$\begin{bmatrix} \text{SPEC} & \text{INDEF} \\ \\ \text{ADJUNCT} & \left\{ \begin{bmatrix} \text{PRED} & \text{'alleged'} \end{bmatrix} \begin{bmatrix} \text{PRED} & \text{'former'} \end{bmatrix} \right\} \\ \\ \text{PRED} & \text{'racketeer'} \end{bmatrix}$$

This f-structure would be the correspondent of all the nominal nodes in a c-structure like this:

(11)

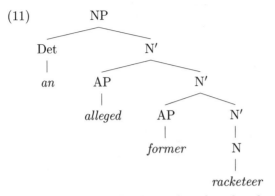

racketeer

But the f-structure is obviously a hopeless basis for semantic interpretation, since the semantic structure is clearly concentrically nested in the same way that the c-structure is: *former* can be regarded as an 'operator' that applies to a descriptive term, forming a new descriptive term that describes things that once satisfied the description provided by the operand (when *former* applies to *racketeer*, we get a term describing entities that at one time in the past satisfied the term *racketeer*). *Alleged* is likewise an operator applying to descriptions: it is applied to entities which someone has alleged to satisfy the operand description. Therefore the order of adjectives determines the semantic interpretation correspondingly: an *alleged former racketeer* is different from a *former alleged racketeer* (even though this latter concept is not as pragmatically felicitous). Each N′ in the c-structure corresponds to one of these descriptive terms in the semantics. When an N′ expands as an adjective phrase and another N′ in this way, it is the adjective phrase that is the 'semantic head' of the parent – even though it does not share its category – while the N′ daughter functions as the 'categorial head'. When the N′ expands just as a noun (e.g., the bottom N′ node in (11)), the N is both the categorial and the semantic head. We can indicate this – informally for the moment – by writing α above the node that is the semantic head, and κ above the node that is the categorial head of each local tree, yielding the following:[5]

---

[5] We label the Determiner as a semantic head, although we do not present a treatment of determiners here.

(12)

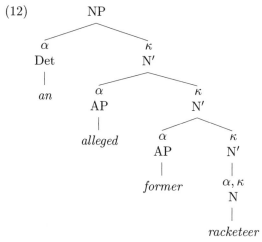

It should be clear that accounting for the semantics of these constructions requires a relationship between c-structure and the semantics that is not mediated by f-structures in the usual way, wherein a semantic representation is derived from the f-structure (Halvorsen 1983, Fenstad et al. 1987, Kaplan 1995). For on such a view, once two of the nominal nodes in (12) have been functionally identified, they cannot have distinct semantic correspondents, which leads to the absurd view that the nominals in the completed sentence structure all have the same meaning. It is hard to see how a reasonable semantic structure could be obtained at all under these assumptions.

As a final introductory example, we return to complex predicates. In the complex predicate constructions of various languages, we find structurally and semantically complex expressions with multiple predicates, and sometimes recursively nested phrase structures, which seem to behave as a single clause, sharing a single array of grammatical relations. In the generative literature, structures of this kind were first described for Romance languages in the seventies (for example Aissen and Perlmutter (1976) on Spanish and Rizzi (1978) on Italian), and have since been identified and analysed in an increasingly wide range of forms and languages, especially recently (see Alsina et al. (1997) for a wide-ranging collection and overview). In LFG the standard analysis is to suggest that all parts of a complex predicate have the same f-structure correspondent, since this is the natural way to explain the observation that the words share a single domain of grammatical functions. The problem then is basically that the semantic and morphosyntactic properties of these constructions seem to call for a structural articulation that is considerably less compressed than the f-structure.

Consider for example the following example from Catalan, presented by Alsina (1997:238):

(13) Li   acabo de fer   llegir la carta
     Him.DAT I.finish of make read the map
     'I finish making him read the map.'

Because of the sharing of grammatical relations across all of the Vs, extensively documented by Alsina, and by many other investigators for similar structures in other languages, all of the verbs in the above sentence and any VPs and Ss they project must wind up having the same f-structure. For instance, normally clitics, such as **li** in the above example, appear with the verb that they are semantic arguments of, but in complex predicate constructions like (13), sharing of f-structures is needed to explain how **li** can appear proclitic on the first verb, while it is really a semantic argument of the second verb. On the other hand, it is clear that the semantic interpretation of these structures reflects at least the linear ordering of the predicates. Changing the order of the verbs changes the semantic interpretation:

(14) Li   faig   acabar de llegir la   carta
     Him.DAT I.make finish   of read the map
     'I make him finish reading the map.'

Manning (1992) and Alsina (1993) argue for a rightward-branching c-structure for this construction in Romance, in which each V is followed by a VP dominating the remaining Vs, as well as any NP or PP objects at the end. If one accepts this, the semantic interpretation also reflects the phrase structure. For example, (15) shows the phrase structure proposed as the structure for the VP of (14a), and sketches the kind of flat functional structure that has been proposed for such cases:

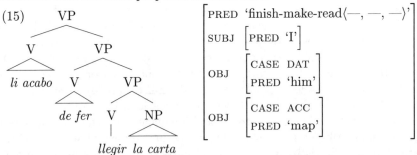

From the semantic point of view, the essential units would seem to correspond to the VPs, not the flat f-structure. That is, the semantics contains subunits such as 'read the map' which correspond to c-structure constituents, but not to f-structures. This goes against Classic LFG, which clearly divided c-structure from f-structure and proposed f-structure as the basis for meaning assembly (Halvorsen 1983). The advantage of this separation is that the theory of semantic composition does not have to cope with the varying word order and constituency that occurs within and across languages. But the problem is that one cannot readily model influences of word order and constituency on meaning, when these relationships are being erased at f-structure, as happens when we adopt the analysis that a complex predicate is monoclausal at f-structure.

One might think that this problem could be easily resolved by setting up some additional projection coming off the c-structure, so that the f-structure could indeed be flattened out, but the new projection would retain the nesting structure that seems essential for the semantics. For instance, we could follow suggestions in Halvorsen and Kaplan (1988) for projecting the semantic structure off the c-structure via a second projection σ. This might give us something like (16).

(16)

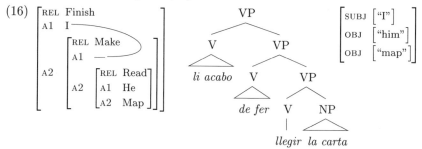

An approach along these lines was proposed by Butt et al. (1990), but, as pointed out by Butt (1995:130), it does not work out, basically because once the information required for semantic composition is scattered across two projections, it becomes quite unclear how to integrate it in a coherent manner. The resulting technical problems are briefly discussed in Appendix A. It is perhaps also worth mentioning that 'semantic projections' as conceived of in Halvorsen and Kaplan (1988) and related works seem to lead to remarkably convoluted notations. To describe natural relationships that involve f-structure and the semantic structure, one needs complicated forms of equations like '$(\uparrow_\sigma \text{ARG2}) = (\uparrow_\phi \text{COMP})_{\phi^{-1}\sigma}$'. This indicates, in our view, that something important is being missed in the design of the formal theory.

The f-structure is also an inappropriate venue for dealing with various other features of verbal inflection and marking. The first verb of (13) is finite, while the later verbs are infinitives. The middle verb is marked by the preposition *de* which is selected by the first verb, while the final verb is unmarked. If the f-structure of all these verb phrases is shared, neither these features nor the necessary feature selection can be represented at f-structure, since these features would conflict.

Various potential alternatives have been proposed in subsequent LFG literature; two of these, ones developed by Butt and Alsina, will be discussed in the next chapter. Some other proposals will be briefly covered in Appendix A, while a short discussion of the treatment of Romance complex predicates in HPSG can be found in Chapter 3.

2   Projections as restriction classes

The current means of dividing information in LFG is via setting up multiple projections as in (16) (Kaplan 1995). For example, as well as the grouping of information in the f-structure that is the range of the ϕ projection, one can introduce a second semantic structure which contains semantic information, as in the example above. This collection of information is the range of the σ projection. Projections are thus locations where information of different sorts is put. We maintain that this 'location-based' conception of a projection that is currently LFG is not the only one possible, and indeed is not the best one for many linguistic problems. It suffers from notational unwieldiness, formal problems, and the inability to manipulate different overlapping subsets of information. It does not naturally support the possibilities of having multiple notions of head and differential spreading, which we have just tried to motivate.

Here we will present an alternative: projections should be viewed as simply groupings of information, that is, subsets. More technically, a projection is a set-theoretical restriction of a feature-structure by a specific set of attributes. Given a set of attributes, such perhaps as the set of grammatical relations {SUBJ, OBJ, ADJUNCT, ...}, which we will refer to as ρ (its exact membership does not matter at this point), and an f-structure f, we calculate the restriction of f by ρ by sifting through f and discarding all those attribute-value pairs whose first member is not a member of ρ; the restriction is what is left. Under this conception the feature-structure contains all the attributes that play any role in the analysis, in one place rather than scattered between different locations, and the projection is formed from the feature-structure by selecting only some attributes, the ones that we want to treat alike for some purpose. We thus replace the use of multiple locations by reference to different subsets of the information in the feature structure. For instance, for the feature structure from (3), repeated in (16), the ρ projection would select just the third attribute and its value – the material shown in the large bold font. A projection, μ, which contains morphosyntactic features like agreement and tense, would pick out just the TENSE attribute and its value.

(17) $\begin{bmatrix} \text{PRED} & \text{`Bark}\langle \frown \rangle\text{'} \\ \text{TENSE} & \text{PRES} \\ \mathbf{SUBJ} & \begin{bmatrix} \mathbf{PRED} & \mathbf{`Fido'} \\ \mathbf{NUM} & \mathbf{SG} \end{bmatrix} \end{bmatrix}$

We suppose that each node in the c-structure tree has a single feature-structure correspondent, where all of the information suitably represented by attribute-value pairs is specified. Then principles specify the sharing of restrictions of these structures between mothers and their daughters. Because these 'projections' (in a sense much closer to the mathematical sense than some of the others current in linguistics) are just sets, rather than kinds of places, different ones can easily share in different ways without interfering with each other. On the other hand, because all the attribute-value information relevant to a node is in one place, the difficulties besetting other approaches to complex predicates in LFG do not arise.

The LFG formalism already includes a conception of what one might call 'negative restriction of an f-structure f by an attribute a', defined by Kaplan and Wedekind (1993) as follows:[6]

(18) If f is an f-structure and a is an attribute:

$$f \backslash a \; = \; f \mid_{\mathrm{Dom}(f)-\{a\}} \; = \; \{\langle s, v \rangle \in f \mid s \neq a\}$$

This says that the negative restriction of f by a is the f-structure that results from deleting a and its value (if present) from f. The concept which we call 'the (positive) restriction of (a feature-structure) f by (a set of attributes) α' is simply the set-theoretical concept of restriction used by Kaplan and Wedekind to define their concept (since f-structures can be thought of as finite functions), and so it does not need an LFG-specific definition; we will notate it as 'f_α', omitting the usual restriction-bar symbol. For example, if f is the feature structure in (17), then:

$$(19) \qquad f_{\{\text{TENSE,SUBJ}\}} = \begin{bmatrix} \text{TENSE} & \text{PRES} \\ \text{SUBJ} & \begin{bmatrix} \text{PRED} & \text{'Fido'} \\ \text{NUM} & \text{SG} \end{bmatrix} \end{bmatrix}$$

Note that restriction as defined here operates just at the top level, and not recursively down through the feature structure.

However, we really find no need to use the full power of restriction in a substantive linguistic theory. Rather, the use for it that we find is always sharing some restriction of one functional structure with the identical restriction of another functional structure. Or informally, we share a certain subset of the information in two structures. For example, if ρ is the set of grammatical relations, then we frequently want to say that the feature structure correspondents of two nodes share the same array of grammatical relations, that is to say that '$f_\rho = g_\rho$'. Therefore, we will propose a special notation for just this operation, wherein '=' is followed by a set of sets whose union is used as a restriction on both sides of the equality:

---

[6]This is only a partial definition of their concept, but it is all that is needed here.

(20) Restricted Equality:

   Where $\alpha, \kappa, \ldots$ are sets of attributes (restriction projections),

$$f = \{\alpha, \kappa, \ldots\}g \quad \equiv_{def} \quad f_{(\alpha \cup \kappa \cup \ldots)} = g_{(\alpha \cup \kappa \cup \ldots)}$$

This is read as 'f and g share (the same values for) their α, κ (and ...)
projections'. In addition, we will use the shorthand $=\{\alpha, \kappa, \ldots\}$ to mean
that $\uparrow = \{\alpha, \kappa, \ldots\} \downarrow$.

   This formal idea gets much of its substantive impact from proposals
about what restriction-classes there are proposed to be. On grounds of
learnability, we would want to assume that these sets are a fixed inventory
supplied by UG. Here are the classes that we find to be motivated so far
by our analyses:[7]

(21) a. κ: X-bar categories like N, V, etc.

   b. β: for the BAR attribute(s) or equivalent in X-bar theory.

   c. ρ: Grammatical Relations (SUBJ, OBJ, ADJUNCT, ...).

   d. α: Argument-structure related attributes such as PRED, and the
      ones we will replace it with in following chapters.

   e. μ: Morphosyntactic features (GEND, NUM, TENSE, etc.)

With these classes we can write a very informal PP-rule such as this for
Spanish 'indirect objects' discussed above:

(22) PP $\rightarrow$ P   NP
                  $=\{\kappa, \rho, \alpha, \mu\}$ $=\{\alpha, \mu\}$

The annotation on the P daughter will cause the sharing of all the feature
classes except for the bar-features, while those on the NP will cause sharing
of the the PRED-feature, and the morphosyntactic features.[8]

   One informal feature of this rule is the duplicated specification of the
'P' category in both the mother PP and daughter P nodes. That these
nodes have the same category is actually mandated by the inclusion of κ
in the shared material. Another is that this rule should be seen as part
of a general schema for expanding [BAR 1] nodes in the X-bar theory. A
partial rendition of an appropriate schema might look like this:

(23) [BAR 1] $\rightarrow$ [BAR 0]   (NP)   ...
                  $=\{\kappa, \rho, \alpha, \mu\}$ $(\uparrow$ CAT$) =$ P
                                          $=\{\alpha, \mu\}$

---

[7]It has sometimes been suggested that morphosyntactic features spread like X-bar
categories, and so μ and κ could be combined as one class. But if one accepts the
analysis of Spanish 'indirect objects' proposed immediately below, then note that μ
spreads differently from κ in this example.

[8]This rule does not share any grammatical functions that might be present in the NP,
such as for example possessors or adjuncts, because at present we have no evidence that
such sharing is necessary, but such sharing could be added if needed.

This says that a bar-1 category expands to a bar-0 one, with appropriate sharing, followed by various things, including among the possibilities that of an NP sharing its morphosyntactic and PRED-features with the mother. But this possibility is furthermore restricted to the case where the mother's category is P. Many of the other stipulations here would presumably be removed by a more substantive theory of feature spreading – for example sharing of κ always seems to imply sharing of ρ – but we will not pause to develop such principles here. Rather we just wish to emphasize that the theoretical innovation of restriction projections allows us to say that different nodes share certain types of information, but not necessarily all information. This can all be represented by showing again the phrase structure for the Spanish indirect object in (7) with each phrase structure node replaced with the feature structure that corresponds to it:

(24)

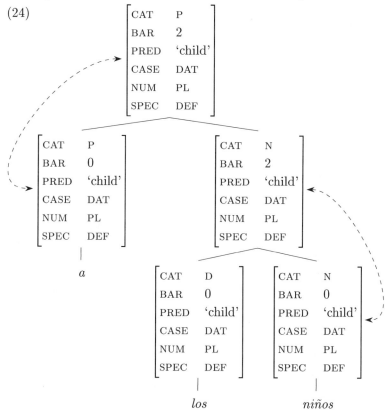

We see that the sharing of the α and μ projections has caused the PRED feature and the morphosyntactic features (CASE, NUM, and SPEC) to spread throughout the tree, while the spreading of the category features is much more limited, happening just where indicated by the dashed lines and arrows.

This example illustrates accurately our proposal, but also suggests a certain practical problem. Although our feature structures are formally just ordinary untyped feature-structures, their size and the lack of any explicit notation showing the extensive sharing of sets of attributes that we propose makes them quite difficult to read when presented in full in the standard notation – even for a very small example like this. One might wish to be able to show just the grammatical relations structure of a sentence, much as in a Classic LFG f-structure (if one ignores the fact that morphosyntactic features were also frequently placed in the f-structure). Fortunately, there is a straightforward way to do this. The restriction operation that we have defined can be viewed as forming a projection of the feature structure (onto the space of finite functions with a certain restricted domain). In particular, in this way we can form a ρ-projection, a κ-projection, and so on. For example, the mapping done by the κ-projection looks like this:

$$(25) \quad \begin{bmatrix} \text{CAT} & \text{N} \\ \text{BAR} & 2 \\ \text{PRED} & \text{'house'} \\ \text{NUM} & \text{PL} \end{bmatrix} \quad \xrightarrow{\kappa} \quad \begin{bmatrix} \text{CAT} & \text{N} \end{bmatrix}$$

While different c-structure nodes will generally have *different* feature structure correspondents under our proposal (although they will occasionally have the same feature structure correspondent in cases such as 'constituent splitting' in Warlpiri as described in Simpson (1991)), many nodes will commonly have the *same* value for various projections of their feature structure. This is because another way to state the effect of the '={ρ}' notation is as a constraint that the ρ-projection of two nodes is the same. Because of the widespread use of such sharing equations, many nodes in the phrase structure tree will have the same value for certain projections of their feature structure correspondent. Thus looking at the equivalence classes of nodes that share the same value for some projection of the feature structure can provide an insightful and compact representation of what is going on.

This suggests the following form of syntactic display. In the first place we have an ordinary-looking c-structure tree, whose nodes are subscripted with an index representing their feature-structure correspondent, as in Alsina (1996). Then there are displays of the projections of the feature structures induced by the tree via the equations attached to syntactic nodes and lexical items. These are standard in form, except that they are pre-superscripted with the indices of the nodes their attributes are shared across, while feature-structures without a phrase-structure correspondent (introduced by morphology for example) are tagged with pre-subscripts (the different position just being a convenient signal not to look for a correspondent in the tree).

In (26), we show again the Spanish indirect object example from (7) and (24).

(26)

$$\kappa: \quad {}^{1,2}\begin{bmatrix} \text{CAT} & \text{P} \end{bmatrix} \quad {}^{3,5}\begin{bmatrix} \text{CAT} & \text{N} \end{bmatrix} \quad {}^{4}\begin{bmatrix} \text{CAT} & \text{D} \end{bmatrix}$$

$$\beta: \quad {}^{1,3}\begin{bmatrix} \text{BAR} & 2 \end{bmatrix} \quad {}^{2,4,5}\begin{bmatrix} \text{BAR} & 0 \end{bmatrix}$$

$$\alpha: \quad {}^{1,2,3,4,5}\begin{bmatrix} \text{PRED} & \text{'child'} \end{bmatrix}$$

$$\mu: \quad {}^{1,2,3,4,5}\begin{bmatrix} \text{CASE} & \text{DAT} \\ \text{NUM} & \text{PL} \\ \text{SPEC} & \text{DEF} \end{bmatrix}$$

In this simple example, for the μ and α projections we have just one equivalence-classes of nodes. For β there are two, corresponding to X^0 and maximal XP categories (here we have omitted any X' nodes, but they could naturally be added). More interestingly, for κ there are 3 equivalence classes of nodes representing the projections of the noun and the preposition, and the determiner (which is just a zero-level category as presented here).

In many cases, it will be convenient to make one further simplification, and represent some of this information as labels on the c-structure nodes, as was traditionally done. In general, the labels on the c-structure tree represent combinations of features on those projections, such as β and κ, which it is convenient to so represent (these will tend to be ones whose governing constraints one might want to compile into phrase structure rules (Maxwell and Kaplan 1993)), while the rest of the projections are represented by attribute-value matrices. This is a convenient abbreviation, but it makes certain sharing relationships implicit, and dependent on the reader's interpretation. Using these techniques, we can return to informational displays rather similar to those used in Classic LFG, as shown in (27), while nevertheless maintaining certain advantages in the machinery under the hood that will better allow us to tackle topics such as complex predicates.

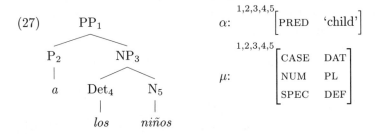

3 Prospectus

In the next chapter we will briefly examine some of the key data that have motivated work on complex predicates and present the popular 'predicate composition' approach to analysing complex predicates in LFG. Then in Chapter 3 we will present our own treatment of complex predicates in Romance languages, and in Chapter 4 move on to applying the present ideas to the treatment of several so-called 'serial verb constructions'. This is a much less-studied domain, but one that holds much evidence suggestive of the need for differential information spreading and multiple concepts of head. After the conclusion, some appendices briefly discuss other formal treatments of complex predicates in LFG and how the ideas presented here can be incorporated into linear-logic-based approaches to LFG semantics.

2

Predicate Composition

Within LFG, the majority of the empirical work on complex predicates has been within the 'predicate composition' approach originated by Mohanan (1988) and Alsina and Joshi (1991), and developed by Alsina (1993, 1996, 1997) focussing on Romance and Bantu languages, and Butt (1993, 1995, 1997), focussing on Urdu (with brief consideration of Romance).

We will begin by presenting some of the key features of Butt's analysis of complex predicates in Urdu. The Urdu data provide a particularly clear illustration of the independence of c-structure configurations from the f-structure issue of whether there is complex predicate formation. This independence provides difficulties for some theories of complex predicates, such as those found in HPSG, but fits smoothly into our approach. From a strictly empirical point of view, Butt's approach works well for Urdu, although we will find some conceptual problems with the details of the formulation. We will then move on to Alsina's treatment of Romance (which is similar in that it was actually an inspiration for Butt's work), where the conceptual problems we find with 'predicate composition' are compounded by some empirical difficulties. Finally, we close with some data from Wagiman (Wilson 1997), which further challenges some of the assumptions of the predicate composition approach.

Aside from these 'predicate composition' analyses, there have been some other proposals for dealing with complex predicates in LFG. There was earlier work within Classic LFG by Simpson (1983) and Ishikawa (1985) which attempted to deal with complex predicates by viewing them as fundamentally an XCOMP-like structure, but with functional control of all grammatical functions rather than just subjects. The approach of Ackerman and colleagues (Ackerman and Webelhuth 1996, Ackerman and LeSourd 1997) resists admitting a predicate-forming operation into the syntax, and hence instead sees the data from complex predicates as a cue to expand the lexicon to allow units larger than single words. Finally, there are various recent pieces of a more formal character attempting to deal with the theoretical problems posed by complex predicates, but, since they do not seem to have led to significant amounts of further empirical research, we will discuss them in Appendix B.

1 Predicate composition in Urdu

Urdu is particularly interesting for theories of complex predicates because it provides a very clear illustration of the independence of f-structure relationships from both c-structure configurations and simple semantic notions. In Urdu, there are two distinct constructions that have approximately the semantics of complementation. But as we shall see, there are two different c-structure configurations that can each be used to express either a monoclausal or biclausal f-structure depending on the construction. Because of this, these constructions impose significant requirements on whatever theory is adopted for complex predicates. An example of each is provided below:

(1) Instructive:
Anjum ne   Saddaf ko   citṭʰii   likʰ-ne   ko
Anjum ERG Saddaf ACC letter.F(NOM) write-INF ACC
kah-aa
say-PERF.M.SG
'Anjum told Saddaf to write a note.'

(2) Permissive:
Anjum ne   Saddaf ko   citṭʰii   likʰ-ne   d-ii
Anjum ERG Saddaf ACC letter.F(NOM) write-INF give-PERF.F.SG
'Anjum let Saddaf write a note.'

Both constructions involve an infinitival (apparent) complement, but the 'Instructive' (involving the verb **kah-**) is found to be biclausal at the level of f-structure, while the 'Permissive' (involving the verb **d-**) has a monoclausal f-structure. That is, the gross outlines of their respective f-structures are as in (3):

(3) Instructive:

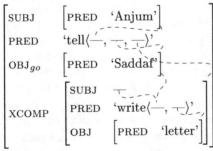

(4) Permissive:

$$\begin{bmatrix} \text{SUBJ} & \begin{bmatrix} \text{PRED} & \text{'Anjum'} \end{bmatrix} \\ \text{PRED} & \text{'let-write}\langle \underline{\quad}, \overline{\quad}, \overline{\quad}\rangle\text{'} \\ \text{OBJ}_{go} & \begin{bmatrix} \text{PRED} & \text{'Saddaf'} \end{bmatrix} \\ \text{OBJ} & \begin{bmatrix} \text{PRED} & \text{'letter'} \end{bmatrix} \end{bmatrix}$$

Saying that the instructive is biclausal means that it behaves syntactically as if there were an embedded clause, which is analysed in LFG as meaning that there is an embedded f-structure (the XCOMP which contains an argument-taking predicate). In contrast, the Permissive is monoclausal, in that it behaves syntactically as if it were a single clause, which is seen to be true in the LFG analysis proposed in (4) in that there are no embedded f-structures containing argument-taking predicates, but just ones satisfying grammatical relations such as SUBJ and OBJ. The Permissive construction is thus an example of a complex predicate.

The examples above illustrate two differences between the constructions. In the Instructive, the infinitive bears the accusative marker **ko**, and the main verb does not agree with the object of the infinitive, while in the Permissive, the infinitive lacks the marker, and the main verb does agree with the object of the infinitive. It has been shown by T. Mohanan (1995a, 1995b) that the generalization governing verb agreement in Hindi is that a finite verb agrees (in gender and number) with the highest-ranked nominative (overtly un-casemarked) NP in the clause, where the subject outranks the object. If there is no such nominative argument, the verb takes a masculine default form. This characterization also applies to Urdu.[1] Butt argues that the agreement in (2) shows that the apparent object of the infinitive is also the object of the main verb, while the failure of agreement in (1) indicates that this is not true there, which supports the monoclausal/biclausal distinction argued for above. Butt (1995) presents further data and arguments from anaphora and control, which corroborate this conclusion. We briefly summarize just the anaphora data here. In Urdu, the reflexive *apnaa* must be bound to a subject while the pronoun *us-kaa* must be free of its local subject. The contrastive binding properties of these words in the Permissive complex predicate (5a–b) versus the Instructive complement structure (5c–d) support Butt's analysis:

---

[1] Which is structurally almost identical to Hindi, to the extent that they are sometimes regarded as being different forms of the same language, the major difference being in vocabulary.

(5) a. Anjum$_i$ ne   Saddaf$_j$ ko   apnaa$_{i/*j}$ xat   lik^h-ne
        Anjum$_i$ ERG Saddaf$_j$ DAT self's$_{i/*j}$ letter.M(NOM) write-INF
        di-yaa
        give-PERF.M.SG
        'Anjum$_i$ let Saddaf$_j$ write her$_{i/*j}$ letter.'

    b. Anjum$_i$ ne   Saddaf$_j$ ko   us-kaa$_{*i/j}$ xat   lik^h-ne
        Anjum$_i$ ERG Saddaf$_j$ DAT her$_{*i/j}$ letter.M(NOM) write-INF
        di-yaa
        give-PERF.M.SG
        'Anjum$_i$ let Saddaf$_j$ write her$_{*i/j}$ letter.'

    c. Anjum$_i$ ne   Saddaf$_j$ ko   apnaa$_{i/j}$ xat   lik^h-ne   ko
        Anjum$_i$ ERG Saddaf$_j$ DAT self's$_{i/j}$ letter.M(NOM) write-INF ACC
        kah-aa
        say-PERF.M.SG
        'Anjum$_i$ told Saddaf$_j$ to write her$_{i/j}$ letter.'

    d. Anjum$_i$ ne   Saddaf$_j$ ko   us-kaa$_{i/*j}$ xat   lik^h-ne
        Anjum$_i$ ERG Saddaf$_j$ DAT her$_{i/*j}$ letter.M(NOM) write-INF
        ko   kah-aa
        ACC say-PERF.M.SG
        'Anjum$_i$ told Saddaf$_j$ to write her$_{i/*j}$ letter.'

It is this kind of data that is fatal for the sort of account involving widespread functional control that Simpson (1983) and Ishikawa (1985) proposed. For if the permissive maintained a biclausal f-structure with an embedded XCOMP, then it would be inexplicable why the binding facts should differ in this way. For instance, in (5a) **apnaa** should be able to be bound by **Saddaf**, who would be the subject of the XCOMP. On the other hand, the binding differences are neatly explained by suggesting that the Permissive is monoclausal at f-structure.

This difference in f-structural behavior co-exists with striking similarities in the possibilities for c-structural realization. Word order in Urdu is fairly flexible, but it does not allow major constituents such as NPs to be split up. At first sight, in both the Permissive and Instructive constructions, the infinitive and its (nominative) object appear to form a constituent, since they cannot freely be separated. Butt (1995:58–74) argues that this constituent is an NP, although, if one adopts Bresnan's recent work on mixed category constructions (Bresnan 1997), it would seem reasonable to analyse this construction with a VP node under the NP. A few of the possibilities are illustrated below, where the (a) examples are the most natural, while the (b) ones are odd for discourse reasons, but grammatically acceptable (Butt p.c., 1997), while the (c) examples are ungrammatical due to splitting up of the infinitive and its object:

(6)   Biclausal Instructive:

   a. Anjum ne [citt^hii   lik^h-ne] ko   Saddaf ko
       Anjum ERG letter(NOM) write-INF ACC Saddaf DAT
       kah-aa
       say-PERF.M.SG
       'Anjum told Saddaf to write a letter.'

   b. Anjum ne   kah-aa   Saddaf ko [citt^hii   lik^h-ne]
       Anjum ERG say-PERF.M.SG Saddaf DAT letter(NOM) write-INF
       ko
       ACC
       'Anjum told Saddaf to write a letter.'

   c. *Anjum ne kah-aa citt^hii Saddaf ko lik^h-ne ko

(7)   Monoclausal Permissive:

   a. Anjum ne [citt^hii   lik^h-ne] Saddaf ko   d-ii
       Anjum ERG letter(NOM) write-INF Saddaf DAT give-PERF.F.SG
       'Anjum told Saddaf to write a letter.'

   b. Anjum ne   d-ii   Saddaf ko [citt^hii   lik^h-ne]
       Anjum ERG give-PERF.F.SG Saddaf DAT letter(NOM) write-INF
       'Anjum let Saddaf write a letter.'

   c. *Anjum ne d-ii citt^hii Saddaf ko lik^h-ne

There is however a striking exception to this: for both constructions, additionally the main verb and the infinitive can scramble together, as a unit, with the infinitive first:

(8) a. Anjum ne Saddaf ko **lik^h-ne ko kah-aa** citt^hii.
    b. Anjum ne **lik^h-ne ko kah-aa** Saddaf ko citt^hii.

(9) a. Anjum ne Saddaf ko **lik^h-ne d-ii** citt^hii.
    b. Anjum ne **lik^h-ne d-ii** Saddaf ko citt^hii.

Butt argues that this indicates that the Instructive and Permissive constructions each have two constituent structures, one in which the infinitive forms a constituent with its object, and another where it instead forms a complex verbal constituent with the main verb. This conclusion is corroborated by further evidence from negation and coordination (Butt 1995:47–51), which we will not review here. Each of these constituent structures is then able to give rise either to the biclausal structure found with the instructive, or the monoclausal complex predicate construction found with the permissive. Butt demonstrates that the f-structural differences between Permissive and Instructive constructions are not affected by the choice between the two available forms of c-structural realization.

The Instructive is appropriately treated as an XCOMP structure. This gives a straightforward analysis of the observed agreement, disjoint reference, and anaphora facts. The analysis is obvious when the infinitive and its object form a constituent, whereas when the infinitive and main verb forms a constituent, all that is required is to introduce the infinitive as an XCOMP and the object of the infinitive as an XCOMP OBJ, which is straightforward, as described in Butt (1995:56–57) and Butt (1997:117–118).

For the Permissive, on the other hand, the analysis involves two main ideas. The first is that both the main and subordinate verbal nodes correspond to the same f-structure, which can be implemented by using the '$\uparrow = \downarrow$' annotation in the places where the instructive structures would have an '$(\uparrow \text{XCOMP}) = \downarrow$' annotation, as illustrated below:[2]

(10) a.

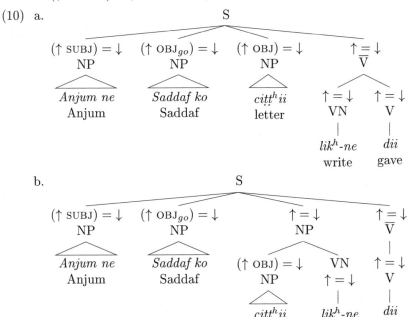

This provides an immediate explanation of the agreement of the main verb with the infinitive's object, and the assignment of a single array of grammatical relations to both the main and infinitive verbs accounts for the other evidence for monoclausality presented by Butt.

But it also creates a problem, which the second idea is required to solve. The problem is that the main and infinitive verbs will both introduce a PRED (note that the main verb introduces an argument, and so cannot be treated as an auxiliary that merely adds a grammatical feature), and under Classic LFG assumptions, PRED values can never unify, and hence

---

[2]Butt (1997) gives the infinitival verb the label 'VN' for 'verbal noun' without being terribly precise about what this means.

the f-structure would be ill-formed. The proposed solution is to introduce a distinction between two kinds of PRED-values, standard ones, which will clash if equated, and 'incomplete', or 'light' PRED-values, which cannot appear on their own, but must be composed with a standard PRED-value.

We believe the basic concept of predicate composition to be correct, and we accept it and use it in our analysis. However, we find difficulties with the mechanisms that have been used to achieve it. Butt and Alsina themselves propose slightly different formulations of the idea. Butt characterizes light predicates as having 'argument-structures' (a reduced version of the semantic representation containing only information relevant for determining whether semantic composition is possible) containing what she describes as a 'transparent event' position, which can be regarded as being essentially a slot into which something must be inserted to produce a well-formed result. The structure for Permissive **de** 'let' is for example (Butt 1995:156):

(11) $$\begin{bmatrix} de \text{ 'let'} \\ \begin{bmatrix} \text{CS}([\alpha], \text{GO}_{Poss}(\{\ \}_{E_T}, \text{TO } [\quad])) \end{bmatrix} \\ \text{AFF}_{+cc}([\quad]^{\alpha}, \ ) \\ \text{ASP}(\text{- - -}) \end{bmatrix}$$

This lexical entry uses an extension of the lexical conceptual structure (LCS) proposals of Jackendoff (1990), which we will not give a full explication of here. But the essential idea is that the LCS contains a 'transparent event' position, marked by an E_T subscript, into which the argument structure of the actual Permitted Event expressed by the infinitive verb will be substituted. For this verb, Butt (1995:155) suggests that "the act of permission be visualized as a metaphorical giving of an Event to somebody", which is realized by analyzing the transparent event argument (what is permitted) as a Theme argument which is metaphorically caused to go to the Permittee.

This permissive argument-structure can only be used with the annotations that produce the monoclausal structure, because otherwise there will not be a full argument-structure to substitute for the transparent event position. The argument-structure for the Instructive on the other hand will not contain a transparent event position, and so can only be used with annotations producing a biclausal structure, since the monoclausal structure will produce bad results due to clashing PRED-features.

While we accept and adopt the idea of combining the argument-structures of the light and heavy verbs, the details of how this is to be specified on the basis of the c-structures and f-structures seem quite unclear to us. Butt (1995:173) adopts an early proposal of Alsina's to reinterpret the standard '$\uparrow = \downarrow$' annotation so that it effects the sharing of all attributes except PRED, which is said to be subject to composition rather than sharing:[3]

(12) $\uparrow = \downarrow$ means   ($\uparrow$ PRED) = function of composition of ($\downarrow$ PRED)

($\uparrow$ ATTRIBUTE) = ($\downarrow$ ATTRIBUTE), elsewhere

This formulation will prevent clashes due to conflicting PRED-values, but there does not seem to be given any fully explicit formulation of the triggering of predicate composition that would indicate when PRED-values are shared and when they are composed, what determines the order of composition if there are multiple possibilities, etc. The formalization of certain aspects of the lexical conceptual structures, such as the assumed difference between coindexation and identification is also less than clear.

Empirically however the Urdu example is extremely important, because it shows very clearly that something like predicate composition exists, and that it occurs both with constituent structures that look like XCOMPs and with those that look like complex verbs. This corroborates features of analyses we will present below, where Romance languages are argued to have predicate composition with apparent c-structure VPs, and the Amazonian language Tariana with apparent complex verbs. We now move on to consider Alsina's treatment of Romance, which reveals some additional difficulties for the LFG architecture in combination with predicate composition, and imposes further requirements that an empirically adequate theory of complex predicates must meet.

2   Predicate composition in Romance

As many have noted, the Romance languages contain a category of 'light verbs'. These verbs take phrase structure complements, which appear superficially to be ordinary VP complements. However, closer examination shows that a light verb and its apparent complement actually combine in such a way as to share the same array of grammatical relations. We will thus use the term 'pseudo-complement' in this case to refer to something that is a semantic argument and a phrase structure complement, but which is not to be regarded as a separate clause nucleus (at the level of f-structure). An example is the Italian causative verb in (13).

(13) Paolo lo farà   scrivere   a Piero
     Paolo it make.FUT.3SG write.INF to Piero
     'Paolo will make Piero write it.'

Note that light verbs are independent words: they retain too much phonological, morphological and grammatical integrity to be able to be regarded as some kind of affix (Kayne 1975, Rizzi 1978).

---

[3]The proposal of Alsina (1993, 1996, 1997) is discussed directly below.

The category of 'light verbs' comprises what are known in the transformational literature as 'reanalysis' and 'restructuring' verbs: a group of verbs covering causatives, permissives, and the basic perception predicates ('reanalysis' verbs), and various aspectual, modal, and basic motion predicates ('restructuring' verbs) (Rizzi 1982, Burzio 1986). The process of one or more light verbs combining with a regular or 'heavy' verb (phrase) was characterized in Relational Grammar as 'clause union' (Aissen and Perlmutter 1976, Aissen and Perlmutter 1983). The similarity between these constructions in Romance and the complex predicates in Urdu and other languages has long been noted, and it has been widely assumed (by Butt, for example) that the same general theory should apply to both.

In the (Western) Romance languages (French, Italian, Spanish, Catalan, etc.), the clearest initial evidence for the existence of light verbs comes from the behavior of clitic pronouns. These languages have various infinitival constructions that behave in the general manner one would expect of complements. In particular, in these constructions, clitic object pronouns appear attached to whatever verb they are semantically associated with (sometimes they precede and sometimes they follow, depending on the form of the verb and the language concerned, but they appear adjacent to the verb and cannot be separated by material such as adverbs or noun phrases). Here we illustrate with some examples from Italian:[4]

(14) a. Piero conosce la signorina molto bene.
    Peter knows the young-lady very well

   b. Piero **la** conosce molto bene.
    Peter her knows very well

   c. Piero affermava di conoscer-**la** molto bene.
    Peter says 'of' to.know-her very well
    'Peter says he knows her very well.'

   d. *Piero **la** affermava di conoscere molto bene.

However, while 'light verbs' take what superficially appear to be similar complement structures, the putative complement manifests various kinds of behavior quite unexpected of a clausal complement. In particular, we notice 'clitic climbing', whereby a clitic pronoun semantically associated with the supposed complement verb can appear cliticized to the light verb instead, as in (15b–c):

(15) a. Maria finisce di batter-**la** a macchina domani.
    Maria finishes 'of' to.hit-it on machine tomorrow
    'Mary finishes typing it tomorrow'

---

[4]We will be using the standard orthographies for all Romance languages, in which proclitics are normally written as separate words while enclitics are written joined to their hosts. We will sometimes set off enclitics with a hyphen for clarity.

b. Maria **la** finisce di battere a macchina domani.

c. **Li** farò correggere
them I.will.make to.correct
'I will have them corrected.'

d. *Farò corregger-**li**

Intuitively, what is going on here is that the light verbs seem to be behaving almost as verbal auxiliaries. This would mean that the sentences in (15) would comprise only a single clause with a single array of grammatical relations. It would then not be surprising that the clitic pronoun, although semantically an argument of the infinitive, could then appear before the light verb. Indeed, its position there would be parallel to what happens in sentences with auxiliaries, where clitics routinely appear before the finite auxiliary:

(16) Maria **l'**ha mangiato
Maria it.has eaten
'Maria has eaten it.'

This idea that we are dealing with a single clause with a single array of grammatical relations is strongly supported by evidence from causatives. When the downstairs verb is intransitive, its 'logical subject' (the least oblique, most agent-like argument) is rendered as an ordinary direct object in a causative sentence; when it is transitive, its logical subject becomes an **a**-marked object (a traditional indirect object):

(17) a. Maria ha fatto lavorare Giovanni
Maria has made work Giovanni

b. Maria ha fatto riparare la macchina a Giovanni
Maria has made repair the car to Giovanni
'Maria had Giovanni repair the car.'

An explanation of this is straightforward within a framework such as LFG or Relational Grammar if we say that these constructions are monoclausal. In general in the Romance languages, one finds at most one subject and one accusative-marked object in a clause. Additional objects are marked with **a**. Under the hypothesis of monoclausality, it is therefore natural that the causee of transitive verbs gets marked with **a**: with transitive verbs there is already an accusative object, and so the causee must be marked with **a**. On the other hand, this result would be quite mysterious if we did not postulate a process of complex predicate formation (one would expect a structure like the English *I made him invite her* with two accusative NPs).

Both Alsina and Butt propose to account for these constructions by means of the same kinds of mechanisms that we previously discussed for Urdu. Alsina however has a somewhat different conception of the details, and Alsina (1997) provides a significantly more explicit account of how predicate composition is supposed to work, which we will now review.

Alsina shares with Butt the idea that light verb constructions are f-structurally monoclausal, and that light verbs are inherently incomplete, although he locates this incompleteness in the PRED-value rather than in a distinct 'a-structure', as proposed by Butt. The problem of clashing PRED-values is met in Alsina (1997) in a way that is substantively the same as in the earlier proposals, although technically a bit different. Alsina argues that both the light and pseudo-complement verbs contribute to yield a derived PRED value for the clause. He suggests that the annotation '↑ = ↓' would thus be misleading, and hence replaces it with a new annotation '↑ $=_H$ ↓', which is defined so as to cause sharing of attributes other than PRED, and to either share or compose PRED-values as required by the circumstances (Alsina 1997:236):

(18) ↑ $=_H$ ↓ $\equiv_{def}$ (↑\PRED) = (↓\PRED)
$$(↑ \text{ PRED}) = \text{F}((↓ \text{ PRED}), (→_H \text{ PRED}))$$

The first line of this definition says that everything except the PRED value is shared between the f-structure correspondents of the upper and lower node. Sharing of PRED is blocked by explicit use of Kaplan and Wedekind's (negative) restriction operator, while predicate composition is controlled by the function F, whose formulation (Alsina 1997:236) is given in (19). F is engineered to compose the PRED of the daughter node that the annotation is attached to (designated by ↓), with that of a sister bearing the ↑ $=_H$ ↓ annotation (designated by →$_H$) when this is appropriate, and effect sharing of PRED-values otherwise.

(19) a. $F(x, \emptyset) = x$
 b. $F(\text{'P}^1\langle a\rangle\text{'}, \text{'}\ldots \text{P*}\langle b\rangle \ldots\text{'}) = \text{'}\ldots \text{P}^1\langle c\rangle \ldots\text{'}$
  where "P*" is an unspecified predicator and "c" is the unification of "a" and "b"
 c. elsewhere, the result is vacuous.

The effect of this annotation is indicated in the following structure for a causative in Catalan (Alsina 1997:237):

(20)

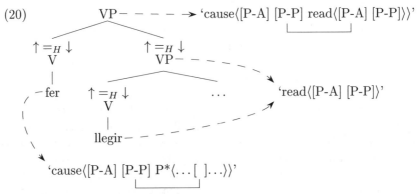

Here the causative verb **fer** has an incomplete PRED-value, the empty position into which substitution is to happen being notated as 'P*' (in the lexical form appearing at the end of the arrow coming form **fer**). This combines with the PRED-feature of the pseudo-complement verb **llegir** to produce the resultant PRED-value for the top VP. A linking theory then associates the argument-positions in the resulting complex-predicate with a set of grammatical relations that are shared across all the VP-levels.[5]

One important feature of this formulation is that it accounts for the fact that complex predicate formation 'respects the tree structure' (Alsina 1997:237), in the sense that when there are multiple light verbs, their composition is guided by the nesting relations in the tree. Alsina illustrates this point with the examples we used previously, which contrast in whether the aspectual light verb is inside or outside the scope of the causative light verb, and thus differ in terms of who does the finishing:

(21) a. Li   acabo   de fer   llegir la carta
        Him.DAT I.finish of make   read   the map
        'I finish making him read the map.'

    b. Li   faig   acabar de llegir la carta
        Him.DAT I.make   finish of read   the map
        'I make him finish reading the map.'

Alsina's formulation accounts for this because in the nest of VP-structures that appear in the c-structures of these examples, each light verb has only one sister bearing the $\uparrow =_H \downarrow$ annotation, which correctly determines how the PREDs are to compose.

But in spite of this empirical success, there are a number of problems. One is that the function 'F' is a significant departure from the range of

---

[5]The '[P-A]' and '[P-P]' notations in the argument-positions represent 'Proto-Agent' and 'Proto-Patient' specifications. These names are taken from Dowty (1991), but the categorical notions they reflect are in many ways closer to the notions of Actor and Undergoer in Foley and Van Valin (1984). The lines joining positions indicate that they are fused (that is, equated).

mechanisms traditionally employed in LFG. LFG standardly employs a very restricted repertoire of techniques to produce the feature structure of a mother node from those of its daughters: the value of a path in the daughter's structure can either be equated to the value of a path in the mother's (by means of an annotation of the form $(\uparrow \xi) = (\downarrow \eta)$, where ξ and η are possibly empty sequences of attributes), or set as a member of such a path (by an annotation of the form $(\downarrow \eta) \in (\uparrow \xi)$). The function F lies outside this spartan inventory, and although it would have to be accepted if there were no alternative, it would be desirable if possible to remain within the traditional techniques of LFG.[6] In particular, if one were to extend the formal inventory of LFG one would want to do it with some general and clean new formal device. The function F and the definition of '$\uparrow =_H \downarrow$' are not devices of this sort. They clearly could have no possible use in the formalism except in the handling of complex predicates. In common with most modern syntactic frameworks, we eschew the use of formal devices and principles which lack any prospect of applicability beyond a single construction type. In contrast, the concept of restriction that we propose is a general device, and, in the introduction, we have briefly shown how it can be used in a number of domains, such as X'-theory and for operator adjectives, as well as for handling complex predicates.

A further reason to reject the introduction of F and $\uparrow =_H \downarrow$ into the formal apparatus of the theory is that they are not in fact used to do anything that cannot be done by unification. In particular, although Alsina argues that composition is a different operation because both of the daughter PREDs contribute to the PRED of the mother, its actual effects wind up looking just like those of unification. Indeed, one can observe that the definition given for F in (19) involves unification. As a result, note that the PRED of the mother in (20) is actually the same as the PRED of the light verb daughter, except that the PRED of the pseudo-complement verb has been 'unified in' at a certain position. The introduction of F and $\uparrow =_H \downarrow$ is meant to address a problem with the substantive assumptions of LFG. Classic LFG had a stipulation, the Principle of Predicate Uniqueness, which ensures that PREDs can never unify. The result is to allow only one PRED-value per domain of fully shared grammatical functions, which makes it impossible to treat the light verb as the semantic head and the heavy verb as an argument, unless new formal devices are added. However, we think that changing the substantive assumptions of the theory is a far bet-

---

[6]We suspect that there may be a significant processing motivation for the LFG approach, for the reason that it guarantees that the values of mother attributes can be computed incrementally, as the daughters are processed, without there being the potential necessity to wait for some arbitrary function such as F to apply to information from all of the daughters.

ter solution to this problem than changing the inventory of formal devices employed by the theory.

Besides these conceptual problems, there is a more straightforwardly empirical one. The $\uparrow =_H \downarrow$ annotation is formulated so as to share all attributes except PRED, but, as pointed out by Frank (1996), there is in fact more than PRED that we do not want to share. Most obviously, each VP-level in these constructions will have its own 'verbal form' features. These will include features marking the distinction between finite, infinitive and (past) participle verb forms, as well as features discriminating between the pre-infinitival prepositional markers (such as **a** and **de**). For example, in (21), the first verb in each cluster is finite, while the remaining verbs are infinitives; the infinitives following forms of **acabar** are marked with **de** while others are unmarked. Alsina provides no account as to how these features are to be controlled. In contrast, we shall see that they are quite straightforward under the analysis with restriction-projections that we propose in the next chapter, where we will encounter some additional features that also do not share.

One possibility for dealing with the verbal form features would be to use the μ-projection of Butt et al. (1996) (suggested by Ron Kaplan). The μ-projection is a projection coming off of c-structure that is similar to f-structure, but shares less aggressively, and contains only verbal form features and an attribute DEP for holding the form features of a VP that is dependent to a verb (i.e., its pseudo-complement). The head of a VP will be annotated so as to share the μ-projection with its mother, while a pseudo-complement VP will be annotated so as to set its μ-projection as the value of DEP in its mother's μ-projection. For example, a Catalan verb such as **acabar** can then specify in the lexicon that its μ-projection has a DEP VFORM-value of INF, and a DEP VMARK-value of DE, as in (22a), and this would be used in conjunction with an annotated partial c-structure tree as in (22b):

(22) a. *acabar* V $(\uparrow_\mu \text{ DEP VFORM}) = \text{INF}$
$(\uparrow_\mu \text{ DEP VMARK}) =_c \text{DE}$

b.

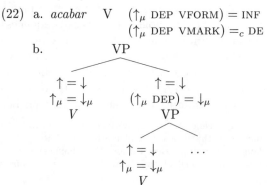

Although this will work, it is notationally rather cumbersome, and involves an unsatisfying overlap in the effects of the theoretical mechanisms employed. Restriction and projections can be seen as alternative means of preventing all attributes from being shared in the same way. It is not desirable for the theory to contain two devices producing such similar effects, especially when there do not seem to be any clearly motivated guidelines for determining which is appropriate in any given situation. One might think to respond to this problem by putting PRED on a different projection from the grammatical relations (perhaps even on the same projection as the verbal form features), but in fact, analyses of this kind do not work out.[7] The problem is that once the semantic information associated with the PRED-feature is placed in a different projection from the f-structure, it becomes very difficult to see how to integrate it with the semantically relevant information provided by the f-structure. In this work we in essence take the opposite approach, using (positive) restriction instead of standard projections.

The above issues are perhaps the most important ones, but there are a number of other problems, both formal and empirical, with Alsina's account. On the formal side, the interpretation of '$\uparrow =_H \downarrow$' is actually quite problematic. Note that, as in (20), this annotation appears on both the light verb and the pseudo-complement VP, and so, in accordance with the definition in (18), both occurrences will be adding a functional equation concerning the mother node's PRED to be solved in the construction of the f-structure. But examination of the function F in (19) shows that this function only 'works' when its first argument is the heavy complete predicate, and the second argument is the light verb. This means that the equation generated by the '$\uparrow =_H \downarrow$' on the light verb in (20) will fail, falling through to the third case: "elsewhere, the result is vacuous". It is unclear how to formally interpret this phrase. One interpretation would be to set the result to [], the bottom element in the lattice of f-structures. But this would only work out if this PRED value were allowed to unify with the PRED value generated by the '$\uparrow =_H \downarrow$' on the pseudo-complement VP – and Alsina's whole approach is predicated on accepting the stipulation that PRED values can never unify. Rather, the interpretation seems to be that because the result is "vacuous" the functional equation should just disappear and not be considered in the solution algorithm. But self-destructing equations are a strange new addition to the ontology of LFG. Note also the new primitive '$\rightarrow_H$' which is used to refer to "a sister node with the head equation". Firstly this significantly extends the set of 'tree walking' primitives provided in the formalism from only being able to refer to oneself and one's

---

[7]Such an analysis was suggested in Butt et al. (1990), the problems with which are discussed in Butt (1995:130), Dalrymple et al. (1992), and briefly in Appendix B.

mother to also being able to refer to one's sisters. But more importantly, it is not even a pure tree-walking operation, since its definition crucially involves reading the annotations on the nodes so that one can select the right sister. A solution that avoids these new devices as well is to be preferred.

Back on the empirical side, Alsina argues that his formal proposal as we have presented it so far still licenses many more configurations than are actually found for complex predicates cross-linguistically, and he proceeds to invent and adopt a variety of principles that would rule out unattested configurations. But we argue that this theory building is proceeding from far too narrow a database, and most of the facts he wants to capture are empirically incorrect. For example, he suggests (p. 240) that "an incomplete predicate cannot appear as a structural sister to an XP bearing a syntactic function", and (p. 241) that through the version of X'-theory he adopts that it is impossible to have a constituent dominating two X^0 nodes, and therefore the only possible phrase structure configuration for complex predicates is the one in (23):

(23)

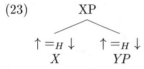

But both of these restrictions are counterexemplified in Butt's analysis of Urdu – see the trees in (10b) and (10a), respectively, and we will see a number of further cases from serial verb constructions in Chapter 4 where the correct analysis appears to be a constituent dominating several X^0 nodes.

3   Wagiman coverbs

Finally, we will outline some data from complex predicates in. This data expands the empirical base with an interesting new type of complex predicate which provides additional challenges that an adequate theory of complex predicates must meet.

In many languages of the Top End of Australia, the functor of a clause is commonly expressed jointly by two words from distinct lexical classes. One is a finite verb (inflected for tense and agreement), drawn from a small set of words with broad meanings, while the other is a word drawn from an open class with more nuanced semantics. We will follow Wilson (1997) in referring to the latter class as coverbs. Two typical examples from Wagiman (a non-Pama-Nyungan Australian language from around Pine Creek, now spoken by about ten people) are shown in (24). The coverb and verb are shown in bold, and in each the coverb precedes the verb (this ordering is common in Wagiman, but other possibilities do occur).[8]

(24) a. jimindirr nganing-gin barri-ba **yurrh-ma**
          knife   1SG-GEN   where-LOC be concealed-ASP
          ngu-ge-na?
          2PL-put-PAST
          'My knife, where have you lot hidden it?'

      b. garra-gu **getj-ja ngan-ge-na**   gahan warren
          money-DAT ask-ASP 3SG.1SG-put-PAST that   child
          wayi-tjjalbu
          small
          'That little kid asked me for money.'

Wilson (1997) argues that these Wagiman verb-coverb constructions are complex predicates expressing a single event, and on this basis demonstrates two further problems within Butt and Alsina's approach.

Alsina (1997:234) states that "two complete predicates cannot compose", and proceeds to build an analysis upon this assumption, whereby predicate composition is possible only when one of the predicates is incomplete, and provides a position (denoted P*) into which the complete predicate will fit as a semantic argument. But Wilson (1997) argues that this assumption is wrong for some complex predicate constructions – and this is the case not only for Australian coverb constructions, but also for many serial verb constructions. In languages of this type, complex predicates are regularly formed in various ways out of complete predicates. Here we will present some evidence for this from Wagiman, and further evidence for the same conclusion from serial verb constructions will be presented in Chapter 4.

A Wagiman verb is not just an auxiliary, but has a predicate meaning and commonly serves as the sole predicate of a clause, as in (25):

(25) garradin **nga-ge-na**   table-ba
      money   1SG-put-PAST table-LOC
      'I put the money on the table.'

But, while coverbs are normally used in association with a finite verb, they are themselves also complete predicates which can be used alone. Sometimes a bare coverb heads a clause when time reference has already been established in a discourse:

(26) **warra-warratj-ja** jilimakgun
      REDUP-dance-ASP   woman
      'The women danced/used to dance/are dancing/....'

---

[8]The **-Ca** suffix on most coverbs is historically an aspect marker, and so is glossed as ASP, but this suffixed form now appears to be the unmarked citation form.

Secondly, there is a productive, though not common, process whereby coverbs undergo zero derivation to become verbs and then take regular finite verb inflections. For example, while a verb-coverb combination like (24b) is more common, one can also verbalize the coverb and express asking as in the following example:

(27) garra-gu **nga-ba-getj-ja-n**
money-DAT 1SG-3PL-ask-ASP-PRES
'I'll ask them for money.'

So, it is also untenable to regard coverbs as incomplete predicates, even though they usually appear with an inflecting verb.

While the verb in a complex predicate sometimes appears to become a semantically bleached auxiliary, as in (24b),[9] commonly both the verb and the coverb jointly express the predicate meaning of the clause:

(28) jahan-gu mahan **dilk-ga** **ginggu-nanda-n-ngana**
what-DAT here   stare-ASP 3SG.1PL-see-PRES-INCL
'Why are you staring at us here?'

In such examples we have two complete argument-taking predicates – a verb and a coverb – cospecifying a single event which has no apparent subparts. It is not plausible to regard this as a case of semantic coordination or subordination. Rather both contribute to the predicate meaning and arguments of the complex predicate, often with a great deal of overlap, as in this case. This argues very strongly that we need the predicate meanings of the coverb and the verb to be able to unify – precisely what was prohibited in Classic LFG.

As well as neither the verb or coverb needing to be incomplete, Wagiman coverbs can add different types of meanings to a verb, and so there cannot possibly be just one marked location in the meaning of the verb (the E_T of Butt or the P* of Alsina) into which extra meaning is inserted. Compare these examples:

(29) a. jilimakgun nung-gin-yi **durdurt bula-ndi**
woman   3SG-GEN-ERG run.PFV 3SG.LEAVE-PAST
'His woman ran away and left him.'

   b. magu **bam-bam-ma**   **nga-bula-ndi**
over there heaped up-REDUP-ASP 1SG-leave-PAST
'I left it heaped up over there.'

In (29a) the coverb **durdurt** specifies a manner of motion, while in (29b) the coverb **bam-bam-ma** specifies the state in which the object was left. Depending on the particular meanings involved, the semantic contribution

---

[9]Although note the English idiom: *I put a question/proposition to her*.

of the coverb can occur in various ways, which would correspond to different places in an LCS representation.

We will not present an account of the Wagiman data here (though see Wilson (1997) for an account using merger of LCS values which is quite compatible with what we propose). However, similar issues arise in the serial verb constructions which we discuss in Chapter 4. We will now turn to developing our own account, beginning with Romance. We show that the single new formal device of (positive) restriction comfortably supports a substantive linguistic theory with multiple notions of head and differential feature spreading, which are the tools needed to adequately analyse complex predicates. Our proposal provides a straightforward solution to both the conceptual and empirical problems we have found in Alsina's account, and generalizes to an interesting range of phenomena in other languages as well.

3

Romance Complex Predicates

In this chapter we show how the core phenomena of Romance complex predicate formation can be treated under a restriction projections approach. The first section explains the basic idea, and the second section then shows how this approach explains the principal ways in which Romance complex predicates appear 'monoclausal'. The final section then briefly compares our approach to work on Romance within HPSG.

1 An analysis via restriction projections

We have already discussed how grammatical relations appear to be shared throughout Romance complex predicates, such as the Catalan causative sentence in (1). For instance, this is what licenses clitc pronouns that are semantic arguments of the second verb appearing in front of the finite causative verb. Manning (1992, 1996b) and Alsina (1996, 1997) argue that in the phrase structure of Romance complex predicate constructions, the light verb takes its 'semantic complement', which we will sometimes call a pseudo-complement, as a VP sister, leading to the c-structure (1b) for the sentence (1a) below:

(1) a. el   mestre fa   llegir   un poema al   nen
       the teacher makes read.INF a   poem to.the boy
       'The teacher is making the boy read a poem.'

   b.

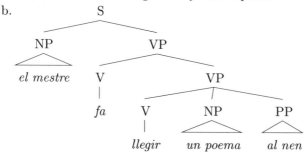

For most people this surface phrase structure is uncontroversial, but recent work in HPSG has argued for a different phrase structure, and so we will actually consider this question in greater detail in Section 3 below. For the moment, however, we will accept this phrase structure as given, and, from this basis, show how our notion of restriction projections provides insight into the main phenomena that are indicative of light-verb constructions in Romance, and of how they can be treated at the feature structure level within LFG.

What should the feature structure correspondent of a Romance complex predicate look like, and what sorts of feature sharing are necessary to achieve it? Because of the extensive evidence for grammatical-relation sharing between the two VPs, Alsina (1996, 1997) wants them to have essentially the same f-structure. We share the overall intuition, but as we have noted in Chapter B, there is a variety of information that has conventionally been included in f-structures which the two VPs do not share. Alsina gives no inkling of how such features, for example, verbal form and prepositional marking, are to be handled, and their presence undermines much of the motivational rhetoric for his approach. Alsina (1997:235) places a '$\uparrow =_H \downarrow$' equation on the lower VP, and argues that the reason that PRED should be treated specially by this '$\uparrow =_H \downarrow$' equation is because its value is "nonunifiable" while all other features have "unifiable" values. But in Romance we have manifestly "unifiable" feature values, which are not being shared, such as the verbal form which is finite present for the higher verb, and nonfinite for the lower verb. However, under our conception of projections, implemented via the positively restricted equality operation, this behavior is not a problem. Features are divided up into certain natural classes and we can directly postulate just the sharing that *is* observed in the data. Our analysis is simply that in Romance complex predicates there is grammatical-relations sharing between the two verbs. We denote by ρ the set of attributes for grammatical relations (SUBJ, OBJ, etc.), and the sharing we desire is easily achieved if both verbs and the VP pseudo-complement share the ρ projection with their mother. This is denoted by '$\uparrow_\rho = \downarrow_\rho$' or just '$=\{\rho\}$', and so the essence of the relationship between the VPs is as in (2).

(2)

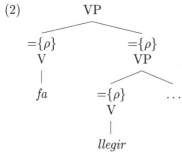

How should semantic information be shared? While the final heavy verb bears the main semantic content of the clause, the meanings of the light verbs are still considerable, and they cannot be represented simply as tense and aspect features, as is often done for verbal auxiliaries. In particular, causative and perception light verbs introduce their own arguments, and in cases where two light verbs precede a heavy verb, the meaning of the complex predicate clearly reflects the order of the light verbs, as seen in the pair of Catalan examples taken from Alsina (1997):

(3) a. Li   acabo de fer   llegir la carta
       Him.DAT I.finish of make read the map
       'I finish making him read the map.'

   b. Li   faig   acabar de llegir la   carta
       Him.DAT I.make finish of read the map
       'I make him finish reading the map.'

It is clear from these examples that the leftmost verb becomes the semantic head of the whole construction. Assuming another set α of semantic attributes, the leftmost verb will then also be annotated with $=\{\alpha\}$. The rest of the complex predicate acts as an argument of this verb, and so light verbs need to have some means of getting hold of the features of their pseudo-complements so as to be able to assemble the meaning of the clause. Indeed this access is not only needed for the purpose of semantic composition, but also for selecting various verbal form and prepositional marking features. As can be seen in the above examples, each verb specifies these properties for the verb below it in the VP-nest. In general light verbs take an infinitival pseudo-complement, but in a few cases this is not so. For example, when the Italian verb **stare** 'stay, stand' is used to form a present progressive, it takes a gerund pseudo-complement:

(4) Ti **stiamo**   **aspettando** da   ieri   sera
     you stay.PRES.1PL wait.GER   from yesterday evening
     'We have been waiting for you since last night.'

Secondly, many verbs take a prepositionally-marked infinitive. For example **acabar**, above, takes an infinitive marked with **de**. That the preposition belongs with the pseudo-complement rather than the governing verb is obvious if we look at coordinated examples where the marker appears on each verb, as in this Spanish example:

(5) Carlos me estaba tratando **de** topar y **de** empujar contra María
'Carlos was trying to bump into me and push me against María.'

For both these purposes we suggest that the pseudo-complement is in some sense an argument of the whole complex predicate, which we will realize by making it the value of the ARG attribute of its mother. Note crucially that ARG is not a grammatical relation, but one of the features on the α-projection. It behaves unlike a conventional grammatical function in that other grammatical relations are shared across it (via the $=\{\rho\}$ equation) whereas normally grammatical relation sharing does not occur across grammatical relations. The introduction of this attribute allows the accessing of the lower VP's information for form-selection, and semantic interpretation, and also for the integration of the argument structures of the multiple verbs.

Finally we observe that there are other forms of information spreading going on. Each verb clearly shares categorial features with the VP it projects, and thus the verbs should share the category projection κ with their mothers. Finally, they should also share morphological form features, like verb form and prepositional marking. For instance, the (maximal) verb phrase in (1b) is finite because the first verb of the complex predicate is. This shows that the μ projection on which morphosyntactic features are placed is also shared. This yields (6) as a revised structure for (1).

(6)

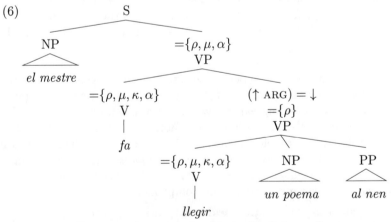

With the introduction of ARG, it is simple for light verbs to govern the form-features of their pseudo-complements. For example, **acabar** from (3) would say:

(7) *acabar*   V $(\uparrow \text{ARG VFORM}) = \text{INF}$
              $(\uparrow \text{ARG PFORM}) =_c \text{DE}$

And similarly, it is no trouble to access the semantics of the pseudo-complement through the ARG attribute. Nevertheless, it remains to implement the effects of predicate composition, at the level of the verbs. What should we do with the PRED attribute of Classic LFG? If each verb had its own PRED and PRED were in the ρ projection then unification of PRED features would fail and the result would be ill-formed. On the other hand, placing PRED in a feature projection that spreads less such as μ would hardly capture the notion that the two verbs combine to license a single flat array of grammatical relations. Moreover, technically, it is quite unclear how completeness and coherence could be checked under such a conception.

The approach we will take is based on some ideas borrowed from HPSG and the theory of grammatical relations presented in Manning (1996a), which in turn are based on a great deal of previous work by Bresnan, Grimshaw, S. Rosen, and others. The proposal is to split the PRED attribute into at least two distinct components, one, LCS, being the lexical-conceptual structure, that is, a representation of the meaning (Jackendoff 1990); the other TERMS, an 'argument-structure' that encodes information about how the lexical item expresses those of its arguments that become 'core' grammatical relations. We will say little about the treatment of oblique as opposed to term arguments here; they could be managed as a separate attribute OBLIQUES (which is similar to Manning's (1996a) proposal, where the argument-list is divided into a term and non-term component), or perhaps they should be handled by some completely different mechanism. Finally, it might also be necessary to introduce an 'instantiation index' to satisfy the role of predicate indexing that assured predicate uniqueness in Classic LFG.

We will not make any specific proposals about the nature of LCS here either, but Butt (1995) argues extensively for a richer semantic representation of complex-predicate formation in Urdu, and adopts Jackendoff's conception of 'Conceptual Structure', and we will generally follow her lead.[1] On the other hand, the value of the TERMS attribute will be taken to be a simple list of positions. This can be implemented in a feature structure Prolog-style as a recursive structure with a FIRST attribute delivering as value the first element of the list and a REST attribute delivering the rest (Carpenter 1992). In this format, adopting for expediency a rather obsolete

---

[1]The notation for the LCS in the feature structure will remain informal and suggestive, but it is quite straightforward to encode the kind of LCS representations that Jackendoff uses within feature structures; see Wilson (1997) for a specific proposal on how to do this. It should be clear that nothing in the present monograph turns on the details of semantic representation.

proposal for the meaning of *kill*, the PRED of this verb would be replaced by:

$$(8) \quad \begin{bmatrix} \text{LCS} & [Cause(X, Y, Become(Not(Alive(Y))))] \\ \text{TERMS} & \langle X, Y \rangle \end{bmatrix}$$

Here shared uppercase italic variables indicate the association between positions on the TERMS-list and positions in the LCS. Such variables are used both for readability and to leave open the possibility of using something more flexible than unification to express the connection. For example, in Appendix A we discuss how one could use the linear logic glue language of Dalrymple et al. (1997).

For predicate composition, what will happen is that the subordinate predicate's LCS will be plugged into an appropriate position in the light verb's LCS, while the tails of their TERMS-lists will be combined, leading to the creation of a single array of term arguments that meet linking theory together. For example, here is one possibility for the lexical entry of a Romance causative verb, suitable for use in the Catalan examples above, or Italian examples that we present later on:

$$(9) \quad \begin{bmatrix} \text{LCS} & [Cause(X, Y, Z)] \\ \\ \text{TERMS} & \langle X, Y \mid \text{—} \rangle \\ \\ \text{ARG} & \begin{bmatrix} \text{LCS} & Z \\ \text{TERMS} & \langle Y \mid \text{—} \rangle \end{bmatrix} \end{bmatrix}$$

This uses one of several possibilities for the composition of the TERMS-lists, unification of the remainders (we are using the vertical bar to separate an element of a list from the rest of the list rather than the next element). If we combine the causative verb feature structure of (9) with that of (8) above, embedded as a value of ARG, we get (eliminating the illustrative decomposition of *kill*):

$$(10) \quad \begin{bmatrix} \text{LCS} & [Cause(X, Y, \underbrace{Kill(Y, W)})] \\ \\ \text{TERMS} & \langle X, Y, W \rangle \\ \\ \text{ARG} & \begin{bmatrix} \text{LCS} & Z \\ \text{TERMS} & \langle Y, W \rangle \end{bmatrix} \end{bmatrix}$$

Here the dotted line connecting $Kill(Y, W)$ to Z indicates that this is the result of identification of this position with the Z value of the ARG LCS. Another issue that is worth mentioning is the treatment of the lower TERMS list. In the notation of both the feature structure for the causative verb (9) and the structure (10), things have been written out so that the upper and lower lists look like distinct objects that share the element Y and their tails. But a snappy way to get both of these identifications would be to just have this equation in the lexical entry:

(11) $(\uparrow$ TERMS REST$) = (\uparrow$ ARG TERMS$)$

Although it is not clear that much of anything hangs on the use or non-use of this kind of equation, there is evidence for different styles of argument-structure composition. Rosen (1989), in particular, argues for the existence of three different techniques, 'transfer', 'full merger', and 'partial merger', which can easily be modelled by the techniques used here ((11) implements full merger). These are not issues that we take up in the overview of Romance complex predicates presented in this chapter.[2]

To complete the analysis, the final ingredient we need is a linking theory, whose job is to equate the positions in the TERMS-list with the values of grammatical functions such as SUBJ, OBJ, etc., the details depending on what theory of grammatical relations is assumed. Alsina (1996) for example proposes that in Romance languages, the top TERM is equated to the SUBJ grammatical function, while the remaing ones are equated to values of a multiple-valued OBJ-function. Under the proposals of Bresnan and Kanerva (1989) on the other hand, the top term would be SUBJ, the bottom term OBJ, and the middle one OBJ$_\theta$. It is beyond the scope of this monograph to make judgements on which of these proposals is the best; assuming for example Alsina's, (10) would be expanded to:

(12)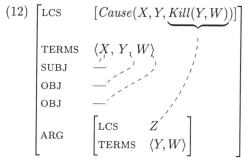

The syntax and morphology will then supply some content for the grammatical relations values, in accord with the principles presented by Alsina for Romance, and in various ways for other languages by other LFG authors.

The presence of both grammatical relations and a structured TERMS attribute may strike some readers as undermotivated, given that in Romance

---

[2]Further exploration of different sorts of causatives and arguments that different languages employ different ones can be found in GB proposals by Marantz (1984) and Baker (1988), LFG proposals by Alsina and Joshi (1991) and Alsina (1997) and in HPSG proposals for Japanese and Inuit in Manning et al. (in press) and Manning and Sag (in press).

languages in particular, the assignment of the grammatical relations is predictable from the structure of the TERMS-list. But beyond their utility in the analysis of complex predicates, there is excellent typological evidence for having these two independent dimensions of clause-structure. In particular, Manning (1996a) shows that one can thereby produce an enlightening account of both 'syntactically ergative' languages and the notorious 'Philippine type', the essential idea being that in these languages it is not required that the SUBJ-value be identified with the top of the TERMS-list. It therefore happens that these kinds of languages often exhibit 'mixed subject' properties, since some grammatical effects are sensitive to TERMS-list properties and others to the grammatical relations.

To summarize the presentation so far, we have provided an analysis of Romance complex predicates which uses the notion of differential spreading. This means that a daughter node can be a head with respect to some classes of attributes (such as here grammatical relations) but not with respect to all attributes. The information sharing relationships we proposed were summarized in (6). We then showed how introduction of an ARG attribute allowed selection of features of the pseudo-complement by the categorial head of the complex predicate. This handles the same data and uses essentially the same structures as have been independently motivated for a μ-projection by Butt et al. (1996), but we consistently use the same mechanisms and attributes for both predicate composition and morphosyntactic feature sharing, rather than needing two unrelated mechanisms. As we have seen, as long as the μ-features are not in ρ, they will not spread between the upper and lower VPs, and so, on our approach as well, verbs can easily select the μ-features of their pseudo-complements. Finally, we introduced a more articulated set of attributes to handle the syntax-semantics mapping in LFG. In particular, our approach through the use of the ARG, LCS, and TERMS attributes allows the effect of 'predicate composition' to be achieved within the system of formal devices traditionally provided by LFG, as just a particular kind of information sharing, rather than as a totally new operation welded on to the apparatus of LFG. These attributes need to be placed in a separate class of 'semantic' attributes α, because they do not spread like grammatical relations, but this approach unifies what is separately being achieved through projections and restrictions in other approaches. Both jobs are done through restriction projections and the use of ARG to allow access to features of the pseudo-complement.

While we in general suppress full structures below, the c- and feature structures in Figure 1 indicate the full picture of what we have in mind for the sentence in (1). The c-structure just shows groupings into constituents (similar to the immediate constituents analysis of 1930s American structuralism) as the category labels have been moved into the feature structure. The feature structure shows the correspondent of the whole sentence. Note that the values of the grammatical relations in the feature structure are correspondents only of the phrasal nodes. The correspondents of head daughters are not directly incorporated into this feature structure (and are not shown in the figure), although almost all the information in them is, through the various feature sharing equations. We could, if we wished, incorporate that information by employing something like a HEAD-DTR attribute, as in HPSG, but at present we see no particular advantage in heading down that route. This difference leads to an important, if subtle, difference between our conception and that of Classic LFG. In Classic LFG, the feature structure shown for the SUBJ in (13) would be the correspondent of the subject NP, the head noun of that NP, and of any intervening N′ projections. In contrast, on our conception, it is the correspondent of only the constituent node that covers the whole subject NP. It just happens that sharing relationships mean that nearly all the feature information in the feature correspondent of the head noun gets copied into the feature correspondent of the subject NP.

2 A monoclausal array of grammatical relations

An analysis along the lines just presented is supported by a whole range of interrelated 'transparency' effects that occur with light verbs which indicate that they are a domain of grammatical relations sharing. The evidence we will consider draws a contrast between simplex clauses and ones with complex predicates in them on the one hand, versus sentences with embedded complements on the other hand. This distinction cannot be suitably captured if we regard complex predicates as basically like other cases of an embedded clause except for some special dispensation that licenses the kind of clitic climbing which we saw earlier. However, we will show that this contrast falls out quite neatly if one adopts the analysis of complex predicates presented above.

2.1 Tough movement

The Romance languages have a construction that looks like the English *tough*-movement construction, shown for example in this Italian example originally from Rizzi (1982):

(13) Questo problema è difficile da   risolvere
      This   problem is difficult 'from' to.solve

However, in contrast to English, *tough*-movement in Romance is normally strictly clause bounded and an example like (14) is impossible:

(14) *Questo lavoro è facile da   promettere di finire   per
      This   work   is easy 'from' to.promise 'of' to.finish by
      domani
      tomorrow

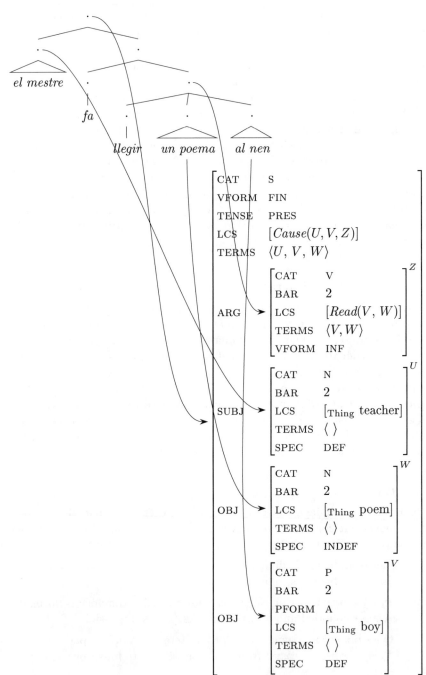

FIGURE 1 Full representational structures

This argues that *tough*-movement in Romance should not be treated as a long distance movement construction, as is often done for English. Rather, we might suggest the following sort of lexical entry for adjectives that allow tough movement:

(15) difficile A   ($\uparrow$ TERMS) = $\langle(\uparrow$ SUBJ$)\rangle$
  ($\uparrow$ LCS) = [Difficult(($\uparrow$ XCOMP))]
  ($\uparrow$ SUBJ) = ($\uparrow$ XCOMP OBJ)
  ($\uparrow$ XCOMP SUBJ LCS) = 'pro-arb'
  ($\uparrow$ XCOMP SUBJ TERMS) = $\langle\,\rangle$
  ($\uparrow$ XCOMP VFORM) = INF
  ($\uparrow$ XCOMP PFORM) = DA

The athematic subject of the adjective is thus construed as the object of its XCOMP, while the subject of the XCOMP is given an arbitrary pro interpretation.

But, just in the case of light verbs, the whole complex predicate seems to act like a single complex verb, and 'long distance' tough movement becomes possible:

(16) Questa canzone è facile da   cominciare a cantare
  This   song   is easy 'from' to.begin   to sing

But given the analysis that we have just proposed of complex predicate formation, the contrast between (14) and (16) follows immediately, without anything further being said. Example (14) will be ill-formed because the verb **finire** will be incomplete, lacking an object, while the lexical entry for **facile** will provide an object to the clause containing the verb **promettere** which will make that clause incoherent. But for example (16), complex predicate formation means that grammatical relations will be shared between the feature structure corresponding to the verb **cantare** and the feature structure corresponding to the verb **cominciare**. Thus the verb phrase **da cominciare a cantare** will yield the partial feature structure shown in (17):

(17) $\begin{bmatrix} \text{LCS} & [\text{Begin}(X,\ \text{Sing}(X,\ Y))] \\ \text{TERMS} & \langle X, Y \rangle \\ \text{PFORM} & \text{DA} \\ \text{VFORM} & \text{INF} \\ \text{SUBJ} & X \\ \text{OBJ} & Y \end{bmatrix}$

This f-structure for the complex predicate interacts correctly with the lexical entry shown in (15), giving a well-formed sentence. One gets the tree shown in (18a), which yields the f-structure shown in (18b).

(18) a.

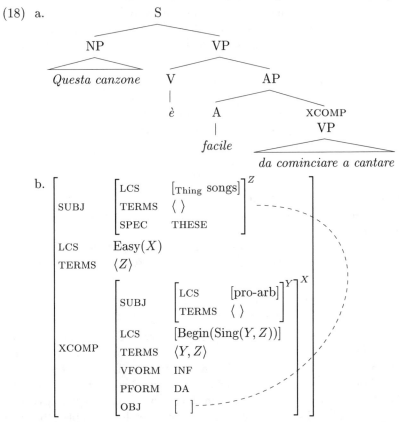

Our conception of complex predicate formation is thus delivering the correct results for free.

2.2 Case marking and word order in causatives

Recall the basic alternation in causativization between intransitive and transitive verbs.[3] When the downstairs verb is intransitive, its 'logical subject' is rendered as an ordinary direct object in a causative sentence; when it is transitive, its logical subject becomes an **a**-marked object (a traditional indirect object), as in these Italian examples:

(19) a. Maria ha fatto lavorare Giovanni
          Maria has made work   Giovanni

      b. Maria ha fatto riparare la macchina a Giovanni
           Maria has made repair   the car   to Giovanni
           'Maria had Giovanni repair the car.'

---

[3]There are other possibilities for Romance causatives that we discuss later.

If our linking theory essentially follows that of Alsina (1996), then these linking results follow automatically. Alsina's theory gives the result that the highest term argument becomes the subject, and that the remaining term arguments become objects, with a rule in Romance saying that objects higher than another object are marked **a**. Under our proposal for complex predicate formation, the complex predicates in (19) will have the fused TERMS lists shown in (20):

(20) a. $\begin{bmatrix} \text{TERMS} & \langle U, V \rangle \\ \text{LCS} & \text{Make(Maria}^U, \text{ Giovanni}^V, \text{ Work}(V)) \end{bmatrix}$

   b. $\begin{bmatrix} \text{TERMS} & \langle X, Y, Z \rangle \\ \text{LCS} & \text{Make(Maria}^X, \text{ Giovanni}^Y, \text{ Repair}(Y, \text{car}^Z)) \end{bmatrix}$

Alsina's linking theory will then correctly make U and X subjects, and V, Y, and Z objects, with Y being an **a**-marked object. On the other hand, if a process of complex predicate formation were not postulated, the case marking frames that occur with causative verbs would be quite mysterious.

   In particular, the GB-style approach wherein the causee argument (V and Y, respectively) is represented as a subject but getting some form of special case marking, not only requires extra assumptions to get case marking right, but it cannot correctly predict word order in causative clauses, as is shown by Miller (1991) for French and Alsina (1996) for Catalan. The crucial data comes from verbs that subcategorize a PP complement, as in these examples from Catalan (Alsina 1996):

(21) a. L'estora, la farem   posar sota   la taula a la   Maria.
       the rug it we shall make put   under the table to the Mary

   b. L'estora, la farem   posar a la   Maria sota   la   taula.
       the rug it we shall make put   to the Mary under the table
       'The rug, we shall make Mary put it under the table.'

   c. Farem   creure /confiar la Maria en   l'atzar.
       we shall make believe/rely   the Mary on/in the chance

   d.??Farem   creure /confiar en   l'atzar   la Maria.
       we shall make believe/rely   on/in the chance the Mary
       'We shall make Mary believe in/rely on chance.'

With a transitive embedded verb, the causee can appear freely ordered with other PP complements, whereas with a verb that only subcategorizes for a PP complement, the direct object causee must precede the PP complement. These facts immediately fall out from independently required linear precedence constraints if the causee is treated as a complement within a complex predicate. However, if the causee is regarded as a subject, then some sort of extraneous fixup must be done. For example, Rosen (1989) suggests a PP extraposition process. This argument justifies the position of the causee in phrase structure that was assumed in (1b).

2.3 Passive

Passivization of Romance complex predicates is restricted, but nevertheless, it is sometimes possible, for example with Italian causatives (Burzio 1986) and Spanish aspectual light verbs. For example, consider the latter:

(22) a. Los obreros están terminando de pintar estas paredes.
        'The workers are finishing painting these walls.'
      b. Estas paredes están siendo terminadas de pintar (por los obreros).
        'These walls are being finished to paint (by the workers).'

An example like (22b) cannot possibly be explained as a lexical rule passivizing just one verb (passive should not be able to apply to *finish* when it is taking a verbal/sentential complement, and this would not explain how the logical object of the rightmost verb ends up as subject of the whole sentence). Rather, the whole complex predicate is being passivized (as evidenced by the passive auxiliary appearing before **terminar**). In a case such as this, we wish to say that the domain of grammatical relations sharing, which is also the domain over which combination of TERMS lists takes place, is also the bounded domain over which passivization can apply. Normally that domain is the projection of a single verb, but with these complex predicate constructions, the domain is larger and passivization can apply over an entire complex predicate. This follows straightforwardly if we view passivization as an operation that applies to TERMS lists.

Under the account of passives of Grimshaw (1990) and Bresnan and Zaenen (1990), passive suppresses the highest term argument so that it does not link to a grammatical relation, something that we might express with an equation like ($\uparrow$ TERM FIRST) = NULL. It is then straightforward how this account extends to our theory of complex predicates. For the active sentence in (22a), we would have the partial structure shown in (23).

$$(23) \begin{bmatrix} \text{LCS} & [Finish(X, Paint(X, Y))] \\ \text{TERMS} & \langle X, Y \rangle \end{bmatrix}$$

Now, this can appear as an active structure, in which X becomes the SUBJ and Y the OBJ yielding the structure in (24).

$$(24) \begin{bmatrix} \text{LCS} & [Finish(X, Paint(X, Y))] \\ \text{TERMS} & \langle X, Y \rangle \\ \text{SUBJ} & X \\ \text{OBJ} & Y \end{bmatrix}$$

Alternatively, this argument structure can undergo passivization, and become:

(25) $\begin{bmatrix} \text{LCS} & [Finish(X, Paint(X,Y))] \\ \text{TERMS} & \langle \text{NULL}^X, Y \rangle \\ \text{SUBJ} & Y \end{bmatrix}$

There is now only one TERM argument to link, Y, which becomes the SUBJ, in accord with Alsina's linking theory, giving us the sentence in (22b).

2.4 Impersonal/Reflexive Passive and Long Object Preposing

Similar results can be seen by looking at the phenomenon of Object Preposing that occurs in conjunction with the impersonal use of the reflexive **si/se** to yield what is sometimes called the Reflexive Passive (see Rizzi (1982) for Italian; Aissen and Perlmutter (1983:369–372) for Spanish). In fact, unlike 'long' passives which are rather restricted (Aissen and Perlmutter 1983:392), this phenomenon is more generally applicable to all cases of restructuring verbs.

One use of the 'reflexive' clitic **si** in Italian is as an impersonal subject marker:

(26) a. Non vi   si dorme volontieri
Not there **si** sleeps willingly
'One doesn't sleep willingly there.'

    b. Si mangiano aragoste in primavera
si eat.PL   lobsters in spring
'One eats lobsters in the spring.'

One might think that these sentences involve **si** filling the subject slot and giving it the semantic content of a PRO$_{arb}$ (unspecified 'impersonal' referent), but in cases like those in (27) where this construction is associated with Object Preposing, such an analysis could not possibly be maintained in either HPSG or LFG (or indeed even in 'Classical' GB: the analysis of Burzio (1986:48) violates the projection principle/theta criterion by suggesting that both **si** and the preposed object spend some time in the subject position).

(27) a. si costruisce troppe   case   in questa città.
si builds.SG too many houses in this   city

    b. troppe   case   si costruiscono in questa città
too many houses **si** builds.PL   in this   city

In (27b), the 'logical object' appears before the verb, and verbal agreement (and the ability to undergo Raising and *pro*-drop: see Burzio 1986:46) suggests that it is occupying the subject position.[4] If this is the case, then

---

[4]The form in (27a) is somewhat of an idealization of the data, as for many Italians this

we would expect Object Preposing to be clause-bound: the principles of most current linguistic theories would prohibit the 'logical object' NP from moving through or occupying a subject position that is getting a thematic role from somewhere. (28b) shows that this is the case.

(28) a. Si propende sempre a pagare le tasse il più tardi possibile.
     si is inclined always to pay   taxes   as late as   possible

    b.*Le tasse si propendono sempre a pagare il più tardi possibile.

If the fronted NP is occupying the subject position, it follows that the **si** in (27b) cannot be a mere marker of an impersonal subject (like **man** in German) but must indicate suppression of the highest theta role (along the general lines of the passive, but always semantically binding it as a PRO_{arb} rather than allowing realization via an adjunct).

Again, restructuring verbs diverge markedly from XCOMP-taking verbs (Rizzi 1982:16), appearing to allow 'long' Object Preposing into subject position:

(29) a. Queste case   si vogliono vendere a   caro prezzo.
     these   houses **si** wants   to sell   at a high price
     'They want to sell these houses at a high price.'

    b. I   problemi principali si continuano a dimenticare
     the problems main   **si** continues   to forget
     'People continue to forget the main problems.'

Rizzi furthermore goes on to show that these apparently anomalous 'long-distance' Object Preposing constructions appear in correlation with the usual properties of Romance complex predicates, such as the inability to pied-pipe the lower VP in cases of *Wh*-movement. Apparent long-distance Object Preposing can require clitic-climbing, in the presence of appropriate clitics:

(30) a. Si vuole vender-gli queste case   a caro prezzo.
     si wants sell-him   these   houses at a high price

    b. Gli si vuole vendere queste case a caro prezzo.

    c.*Queste case si vogliono vendergli a caro prezzo.

    d. Queste case gli si vogliono vendere a caro prezzo.

This provides quite strong evidence that the possibility of Object Preposing is a consequence of the complex predicate formation that licenses clitic climbing.

Under our analysis of complex predicates, such data is amenable to a similar analysis to passives. Object preposing is a process that suppresses

---

sentence is fairly bad with a singular verb form (see Burzio 1986:76, fn. 31). We accept Burzio's analysis that the related sentences where there is agreement with the 'logical object' but where this NP appears at the end of the sentence follow from the general possibility of Subject Postposing in Italian.

the highest argument on the TERMS list while binding it to an arbitrary pro interpretation. Just as with the passive, this operation will be local in its effect to one verb except in cases of complex predicate formation, where a combined TERMS list results.

2.5 Adverb scope

Pollard and Sag (1987) suggest that adjuncts must appear within the maximal projection of the lexical head which they modify, not embedded in any other maximal projection (except that relative clauses can be structural sisters of the NPs they modify). This requirement is too severe, and it appears that adverbs can participate in long distance dependencies (Manning 1992, Pollard and Sag 1994), but nevertheless, we can maintain the principle that an adjunct cannot modify a higher clause than the one that it is embedded in:

(31) a. ?I'm confident that we will be highly able to solve this problem.
          $\neq$ 'I'm highly confident that we will be able to solve this problem.'
      b. I made him climb down without hesitating into the pit of vipers.
          $\neq$ 'Without hesitating I made him climb down into the pit of vipers.'

It is thus initially surprising with Romance complex predicates that such modification of the 'main' verb from 'downstairs' is possible. The following examples are from Catalan (Alsina 1996 and p.c., 1992):

(32) a. He   fet   beure el vi   a contracor   a la Maria.
          I have made drink the wine against x's will to the Mary
          'I have made Mary drink the wine against her/my will.'
      b. Volia   tastar   amb molt d'interès la cuina tailandesa
          I wanted to taste with much interest the cuisine Thai
          'I wanted to taste Thai food with much interest.'
          (with *with much interest* most naturally modifying *want*)

Since there is no phrase-structural reason not to regard the embedded complement as a VP, it thus seems that the phrase-structural notion of 'maximal projection' is not the right way to capture adverb scope. Rather, if we regard complex predicates as a syntactically monoclausal domain of grammatical relation spreading, the right notion is that adjuncts must scope within the domain in which grammatical relations are shared, and this is the result given by the standard LFG treatment of adjuncts via the ADJUNCT grammatical function. For simple predicates this definition and the previous definition coincides, but this new definition correctly groups simple clauses and complex predicate clauses together against multiclausal sentences. The prediction is that an adverb appearing inside a complex predicate will be able to modify any semantically appropriate verb within the complex predicate, and this seems to be correct.[5]

2.6 Auxiliary selection in Italian

The basic facts about the alternation of the perfective auxiliary in Italian between **avere** 'have' and **essere** 'be' are well known (see Rizzi 1982 and especially Burzio 1986). It will be sufficient for present purposes to know that **essere** is used with unaccusative verbs, giving basic facts such as these:

(33) a. Piero ha/*è mangiato con noi
       'Piero has/*'is' eaten with us.'
    b. Piero ha/*è voluto questo libro
       'Piero has/*'is' wanted this book.'
    c. Piero *ha/è venuto con noi
       'Piero *has/'is' come with us.'

With restructuring verbs that take **essere** as an auxiliary, one always gets this auxiliary, even in the presence of evidence of complex predicate formation. But observe what happens when a restructuring verb that takes **avere** as its auxiliary, like **volere** in (33b), takes a verbal complement:

---

[5] Alex Alsina (p.c., 1992) supplies some further Catalan judgements that support this position. It is a well-known fact that 'restructuring' cannot occur when the embedded clause is negated. Thus while we can form a complex predicate that allows clitic climbing in the usual way as in (i):

(i) L'he volgut entendre.
    'I have wanted to understand it.'

if the embedded verb is negated, it must be in a normal verbal complement and hence clitic climbing is impossible as is shown in (ii):

(ii) *L'he volgut no entendre.
     'I have wanted to not understand it.'

We thus predict that an adverb embedded in the complement clause should be able to take wide scope (scope over the higher verb) in (i) but not in (ii), and that indeed seems to be the case, as is shown by using the adverbial phrase *moltes vegades* 'many times' which is here only semantically compatible with modifying **volgut** 'wanted':

(iii) He volgut entendre moltes vegades aquest problema.
      'I have wanted to understand this problem many times.'
(iv) *L'he volgut no entendre moltes vegades.

The sentence (v) with the adverbial phrase at the end is much better, but in this case we can regard the adverb as being a sister of the higher verb.

(v) ?He volgut no entendre aquest problema moltes vegades.
    'I have wanted to not understand this problem many times.'

While negating an infinitive is apparently never particularly felicitous in Catalan, the contrasts between (iii) and (iv) and (iv) and (v) strongly support our analysis. Incidentally note that an adverb embedded in the lower clause can apparently take wide scope regardless of whether clitics climb or not. This would support the position of Moore (1990) that clitic climbing in Spanish and Catalan is basically always optional in cases of restructuring.

(34) a. Piero ha/*è voluto mangiare con noi
'Piero has/*'is' wanted to eat with us.'

    b. Piero ha/è voluto venire con noi
'Piero has/'is' wanted to come with us.'

Avere is always good, but if the downstairs verb would normally take **essere**, then **essere** is also possible. Importantly, it seems that **essere** is necessarily used as the auxiliary when restructuring has occurred (and not otherwise).[6] For example, VP pied-piping accompanying *Wh*-movement, which prevents complex predicate formation prevents the auxiliary change (35a) and clitic climbing is impossible without the auxiliary change having occurred (35b).

(35) a.   La casa paterna, tornare alla quale Maria
        the house paternal return.INF to the which Maria

$$\left\{ \begin{array}{l} \text{avrebbe} \quad \text{voluto} \\ \text{have.COND wanted} \\ \text{*sarebbe} \quad \text{voluta} \\ \text{'be'.COND wanted} \end{array} \right\} \begin{array}{l} \text{già} \quad \text{da} \quad \text{molto tempo, ...} \\ \text{already since much time} \end{array}$$

'Her paternal home, to which Maria would have wanted to go back for a long time, ...'

    b. *?Maria **ci** ha dovuto venire molte volte
'Maria has had to come there many times.'

We thus have the result that in cases of restructuring where the light verb would take **avere**, the choice of auxiliary is being determined by whether the righthand verb would take **avere** or **essere**. This result seems completely general. Rizzi (1982:22–23) demonstrates that no matter how many restructuring verbs occur between the auxiliary and the rightmost verb, it is still the rightmost verb that determines auxiliary selection:[7]

(36) a. Maria li avrebbe voluti andare a prendere lei stessa
        [avere] [essere] [avere]
'Maria would have (**avere**) wanted to go to get them herself.'

    b. Maria ci sarebbe dovuta cominciare ad andare
        [avere] [avere] [essere]
'Maria would have (**essere**) had to begin to go there.'

    c. Maria li avrebbe potuti stare per andare a prendere
        [avere] [essere] [essere] [avere]
        lei stessa

---

[6]Recall that restructuring is optional with these modal and aspectual verbs in Italian.

[7]The auxiliaries that verbs would normally select are shown beneath them in these examples. Note that each example has a climbed clitic proving that restructuring has taken place and the auxiliary shown is in each case the only choice possible.

'Maria would have (**avere**) been able to be on the point of going to get them herself.'

The basic generalization is that verbs that lack an external argument take the auxiliary **essere**. If we accept that this is a property that is being evaluated with respect to the LCS and TERMS attributes, it is actually quite natural that this information will be determined by the righthand verb: this verb will specify whether its highest argument is external or not, and this information is then just inherited in cases of complex predicate formation with restructuring verbs (restructuring verbs just inherit the TERMS list of their pseudo-complement without making any changes). It is in this sense that light verbs seem to behave almost like auxiliary verbs. Slightly informally, we could then say that auxiliary selection is (partially) determined by the following implication:[8]

(37) ($\uparrow$ TERMS FIRST EXTERNAL) $= - \rightarrow$ ($\uparrow$ ESSERE) $= +$

Here ESSERE is a morphological feature (in the μ projection) which says to use the auxiliary **essere** rather than the default **avere**. This feature will indirectly determine the choice of auxiliary, via these equations on the forms of the perfective auxiliary:

(38) a. **essere** V ($\uparrow$ ARG ESSERE) $=_c +$
    b. **avere** V $\sim$($\uparrow$ ARG ESSERE)

What then of the light motion verbs that always take **essere**? We suggest that they carry a direct specification asking for the auxiliary **essere**:

(39) andare V ($\uparrow$ LCS) $= [Go(X, Y)]$
         ($\uparrow$ ESSERE) $= +$

This specification will achieve the result of mandating **essere** if the first light verb is a motion verb (because the μ projection will be shared with the maximal VP), while it will have no effect when a motion verb appears later in a sequence of light verbs, because there is no spreading of morphosyntactic features between a pseudo-complement and its mother. That this gives the correct predictions can perhaps be made clearer by examining these schematic diagrams of how the spreading proceeds:

---

[8]See Andrews and Manning (1993) for a discussion of incorporating conditionals into LFG.

(40) a. $\rightarrow(\uparrow$ ARG ESSERE$) = +$

$$
\begin{array}{cc}
& \text{VP} \\
\diagup & \diagdown \\
\underset{\substack{\text{V} \\ | \\ \textit{voluto}}}{=\{\mu\}} & \underset{\substack{\text{VP} \\ | \\ (\uparrow \text{TERMS}) = \langle[\text{EXTERNAL} \quad -]^X\rangle}}{=\{\rho, \{\text{TERMS}\}\}} \\
& \quad\quad\quad\quad \text{V} \\
& \quad\quad\quad\quad | \\
& \quad\quad\quad\quad \textit{venire}
\end{array}
$$

b.

$$
\begin{array}{cc}
& \text{VP} \\
\diagup & \diagdown \\
\underset{\substack{(\uparrow \text{ARG ESSERE}) = + \\ \text{V} \\ | \\ \textit{andato}}}{=\{\mu\}} & \underset{\substack{\text{VP} \\ | \\ (\uparrow \text{TERMS}) = \langle[\text{EXTERNAL} \quad +]^X, Y\rangle \\ \text{V}}}{=\{\rho, \{\text{TERMS}\}\}} \\
& \quad\quad\quad\quad \diagup\diagdown \\
& \quad\quad\quad\quad \textit{a prendere il latte}
\end{array}
$$

So, again, differential notions of spreading – TERMS lists that are shared throughout the complex predicates, while morphological features are local to a single phrasal projection – is central to the success of this account.[9]

2.7   Summary

This section has briefly outlined how the major features of Romance complex predicates can be simply and naturally accounted for under the treatment we have proposed. There are, however, many issues that we have not dealt with here, including the finer points of clitic placement, interesting variations in syntactic behavior within the Romance languages, and variations in causative structure between having a term and an oblique causee. Some of these issues were dealt with in more detail in our earlier work (Andrews and Manning 1993), others are dealt with much more fully elsewhere (Zubizarreta 1985, Rosen 1989, Rosen 1990, Alsina 1996, Frank 1996, Miller and Sag 1997, Abeillé et al. in press). Nevertheless, we believe that the framework presented here provides a suitable base on which accurate formal accounts of all such phenomena can be built. However, we will not undertake this task here, but will conclude this chapter with

---

[9] And this success is in general hard won. These auxiliary facts have been a recurring problem in the literature, and are commonly gotten wrong (Andrews and Manning 1993), set aside (Monachesi 1995) or the fact that only the first auxiliary counts is simply stipulated in the text (Butt 1995).

a brief comparison between our approach and work on Romance complex predicates within HPSG.

3 Similarities and contrasts with HPSG

Our proposal of differential information spreading for LFG is in many ways consonant with work within HPSG (Pollard and Sag 1994). In particular, we have argued for projections as groupings of information within the feature structure correspondent of a node, rather than as different places where information of a certain type from all nodes is put. This mirrors the architecture of HPSG where a *sign* corresponds to each node, and it is divided into parts representing phonology, morphology, syntax, and semantics. The ability to define different projections as groupings of information has as its HPSG analog the articulation of the geometry of the sign, to provide groupings like PHONOLOGY or CONTENT.[10] Finally, our notion of a TERMS list is actually quite close to the ARG-ST list of recent HPSG (Miller and Sag 1997, Manning et al. in press). In this section we will thus briefly discuss how our work differs from HPSG. As well as 'compatibility' with existing work in LFG, we feel that it is of some importance that our approach maintains a certain notational simplicity, which has long been an appealing characteristic of LFG for purposes such as pedagogy and descriptive linguistics. The theory is also more frugal and constrained in the sense that we have avoided the introduction of the complex relational constraints often used in HPSG (as was discussed earlier). But beyond that, there are some important differences of perspective and resulting empirical predictions between our work and HPSG work on complex predicates, which we discuss briefly here.[11]

Papers by Abeillé, Godard, Miller and Sag (Abeillé and Godard 1994, Miller and Sag 1997) on French and Monachesi (1993, 1995) on Italian have developed an HPSG approach to complex predicates centred around an operation of *argument composition* – or in categorial grammar terms, division categories – whereby a light verb combines with a lexical complement verb, and inherits its complements. In essence, a light verb has a lexical entry like (41):

$$(41) \quad \begin{bmatrix} \text{CAT} & \text{V} \\ \text{SUBJ} & \langle \text{NP} \rangle \\ \text{COMPS} & \langle \text{V}[\text{COMPS} \;\; \boxed{1}] \rangle \oplus \boxed{1} \end{bmatrix}$$

This says the light verb takes as complements another verb, from which

---

[10]Our proposal is in theory more flexible, allowing definition of arbitrary overlapping projections, but we have not shown that this offers any compelling descriptive advantage.
[11]This discussion is necessarily brief. Some of these topics are covered in greater depth in Manning (1996b); others await fuller treatment elsewhere.

it inherits a complements list and other complements as specified by that inherited list. This analysis leads these authors to argue that complex predicate constructions actually have a flat phrase structure in the Romance languages. In this section, we in contrast suggest that the arguments that they muster are in general not about phrase structure but functional structure (to couch the discussion in LFG terms). Thus they are correctly captured in the analysis we propose in which an entire complex predicate shares a domain of grammatical relations. On the other hand, we argue that there is good evidence from Romance that the phrase structure of complex predicates is not flat, and even stronger evidence if one looks crosslinguistically, that one would not want to demand a flat phrase structure in all cases of complex predicate formation.

Abeillé and Godard (1994, 1996) – henceforth A&G – seek to show that the rightward branching phrase structure for French tense auxiliaries shown in (42b), that we have used for Romance complex predicates in this study and which is widely adopted in general, is wrong, and that rather we should adopt a flat analysis for this construction as shown in (42c).

(42) a. Je vous   ai   apporté des bonbons
        I   you.DAT have brought candy
        'I have brought you sweets.'

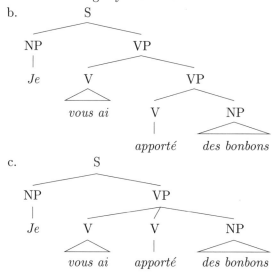

Abeillé and Godard (1994) present many of their arguments as framework-independent arguments in favour of a flat structure, but, in fact, they are not. Several of their supposedly framework-independent arguments are clearly not applicable to an LFG analysis of phrase structure. Indeed it is unclear whether they are arguments about phrase structure at all, or whether they are really just showing the monoclausality of French periphrastic tenses. To gain a broader context on these issues, we would wish to consider these matters not merely within the context of French tense auxiliaries but within the larger domain of Romance complex predicates in general (A&G suggest that "the core cases of **faire** illustrate the same structure" and similar flat structures have been employed by Monachesi (1993) for restructuring verbs in Italian).

3.1 Lack of VP movement, deletion, and pronominalization

Their first argument is that while the infinitival VP complement of regular complement-taking verbs can be pronominalized, (unfelicitously?) deleted, or can appear separately (43), such structures are not possible with the putative VP complement of tense auxiliaries, as shown in (44).

(43) a. Jean peut venir, mais il ne le veut pas
'Jean can come but he doesn't want it.'

b. Marie a voulu visiter le musée, mais moi, je n'ai pas voulu.
'Marie wanted to visit the museum, but me, I didn't want to.'

c. Que veut-elle? Partir.
'What does she want? To go away.'

(44) a. *Jean n'est pas arrivé hier à l'heure au rendez-vous, mais Marie l'est.
'Jean didn't arrive on time at the meeting yesterday, but Marie did.'

b. *Marie a visité le musée, mais moi, je n'ai pas.
'Marie visited the museum, but me, I didn't.'

c. *Qu'a-t-elle? Vendu ses livres.
'What has she? Sold her books.'

Thus French periphrastic tenses do not provide the kind of classic arguments for a rightward-branching VP structure that have been developed for English. A&G take this contrast to suggest that the phrase structure of French tense auxiliaries is fundamentally different, but we should be careful to distinguish an absence of evidence from evidence of absence. These observations should be linked up with observations on Romance restructuring constructions in general. The same kind of prohibitions on movement, pronominalization, and deletion are found with the complement of light verbs in Italian (Rizzi 1978). Since restructuring is optional with most light verbs, we would expect processes of complement pronominalization, deletion or separation to occur when these verbs are used as main verbs, but for these processes not to cooccur when other diagnostics of complex predicate formation are present. As we have seen, two diagnostics of complex predicate formation in Italian are clitic climbing and that the choice of the perfective auxiliary reflects the transitivity of not the light verb but the following heavy verb. Italian has various constructions such such as VP pied-piping accompanying *Wh*-movement (45a) and cleft formation (45b) that can left-dislocate an infinitival VP that is the complement of a modal or aspectual verb:

(45) a. Questi argomenti, [a discutere dei quali] verrò al più presto, mi sembrano molto interessanti.
  'These topics, to discuss (on) which, I will come as soon as possible, seem to me very interesting.'

 b. E' [ad arretrare vistosamente] che la truppe hanno cominciato.
  'It is to draw back considerably that the troops have begun.'

However, this is only possible if the modal or aspectual is acting as a regular, heavy, infinitival-complement-taking verb. As Rizzi (1978) discusses, such left dislocations are inconsistent with diagnostics of complex predicate formation such as clitic climbing (46a) or auxiliary change (46b). Since these constructions are possible only with **volere** acting as a main (heavy) verb, there cannot be an auxiliary change in (46b).

(46) a. *Questi argomenti, a parlare dei quali ti verrò al più presto, ...
  'These topics, to talk with you about which I will come as soon as possible, ...'

 b. *E' [ad arretrare vistosamente] che la truppe sono cominciato.
  'It is to draw back considerably that the troops 'are' begun.'

Thus we note that in Italian there is evidence for an infinitival VP serving as complement to modal and aspectual verbs, and for its ability to appear separately when fronted. Nevertheless, we see that this possibility cannot be combined with complex predicate formation. Now one possibility is that this difference is to be accounted for by proposing a radically different phrase structure in the cases where complex predicate formation has taken place, as A&G propose. But we would prefer to suggest that this is instead to be accounted for simply by showing that VP topicalization of this sort is inconsistent with complex predicate formation (quite independently of any choices of phrase structure for verbal complementation).[12]

There are quite straightforward approaches within LFG to explaining why these constructions are inconsistent with complex predicate formation. In a sentence like (45a), the displaced pied-piped material would have a discourse function as the FOCUS of the clause (Bresnan and Mchombo 1987). If we suppose that possession of a discourse function is inconsistent with

---

[12]A&G (p. 159) indeed seem to realize the weakness of this argument, noting that:
> There may well exist independent reasons for which each of these constructions is impossible. Yet, it must be acknowledged that the structure proposed [the rightward-branching structure] is not supported by syntactic tests.

sharing of grammatical relations (via an $=\{\rho\}$ equation) then this alone is sufficient to rule out complex predicate formation in this case. Another similar way of thinking of this restriction is to observe that the focused material would need to be identified with its role in the clause by means of a functional uncertainty expression (Kaplan and Zaenen 1989). If the landing sites for such expressions are restricted to grammatical relations (as seems linguistically plausible), then there is no appropriate functional uncertainty path for a VP psuedocomplement, since it does not bear an in-clause grammatical relation, but rather is part of a domain over which grammatical functions are shared (Alsina 1993:240). Similarly the clefted material will gain a grammatical function in the matrix clause, and complex predicate formation will be blocked.[13]

3.2 Bounded dependencies

Other arguments of A&G are even more clearly things that would depend on f-structure in LFG. A&G observe that a sequence of a tense auxiliary and a following verb (phrase) functions in some sense as a single clause, rather than as clausal embedding in situations like *tough* constructions and à infinitival relative clauses. So even though French *tough*-movement and infinitival relatives are clause bounded (as in Italian and Spanish – see Section 2.1), they can occur with an auxiliary plus main verb sequence:.

(47) On vient de me donner un travail **à avoir terminé** pour demain sans faute.
'Someone has just given me a job that has to be finished before to-morrow without fail.'

However, these arguments crucially depend on the assumption that the distinction between monoclausal complex predicate constructions and regular multiclause complementation constructions cannot be captured unless they are given different phrase structures. In a framework such as LFG, the distinction at hand is clearly most appropriately captured at the level of the feature structure by saying that French periphrastic tenses (and light verb constructions in Romance more generally) have a monoclausal array of grammatical relations, whereas regular VP-complement constructions have a representation that is multiclausal. This is in line with the analysis of Italian *tough*-movement that was presented in Section 2.1. But these different feature structure representations only weakly constrain possible surface phrase structure representations for these structures. In particular,

---

[13] A similar approach could be applied to *le*-pronominalization, but since, as Kayne (1975:299) notes, *le*-pronominalization is not accepted or is marginal for a variety of clausal-complement-taking verbs, the failure of *le*-pronominalization could easily be for yet other reasons.

they do not preclude a rightward-branching source for complex predicate constructions.

3.3 In favour of the right branching analysis: Coordination

In this section we briefly present evidence from coordination for a rightward-branching phrase structure for French tense auxiliaries. This argument can also be extended to other cases of Romance complex predicates. The facts that we consider in this section come from Kayne (1975:97)). With simplex verb forms, a clitic cannot have wide scope over two conjuncts. The clitic must be repeated as shown in the examples below:

(48) a. Paul **te** bousculera et **te** poussera contre Marie
          'Paul will bump into you and push you against Marie.'
      b. *Paul **te** bousculera et poussera contre Marie

However, in compound tenses, clitic wide scope becomes possible:[14]

(49) a. Paul **m**'a bousculé et poussé contre Marie
          'Paul bumped into me and pushed me against Marie.'
      b. Paul **l**'a insulté et mis à la porte
          'Paul insulted him and threw him out.'

Here the clitic is and must be interpreted as also being an argument of the second verb (which subcategorizes for a direct object).

It is very hard to make sense of this contrast between simple and compound verb tenses under the flat structure proposal of A&G. A&G do not provide an explicit account of this data but suggest that it is an instance of non-constituent coordination, parallel to an example like (50), and that there is "a flat structure for the VPs ... with the Aux taking as complement the concatenation of the two complement lists".

(50) Paul donnera un livre à Gilles et un disque à Henriette.
      'Paul will give a book to Gilles and a record to Henriette.'

But the construction in (49) does not seem like non-constituent coordination to native speakers. Additionally, it is hard for us to see how any gapping or interpretation scheme could allow the sentences in (49) while correctly ruling out – in a principled manner – the simpler sentence in (48b). Moreover, note that the construction we are dealing with is not an allowed type of nonconstituent coordination in English. Compare again the examples in (49) and their English translations. Note how in the English translation, *me* and *him* respectively must be repeated in each conjunct for the correct reading to be obtained.

---

[14]Of course, possible does not mean necessary; repeating the clitics and auxiliaries is also possible: *Paul m'a bousculé et m'a poussé contre Marie*. Such a sentence would be analyzed as (maximal) VP conjunction in a way exactly parallel to example (48a).

However, we can make perfect sense of the ungrammaticality of (48b) if we assume the rightward-branching structures shown in (51). In the compound tense form (51a), the object clitic is higher up and necessarily has scope over all conjuncts, whereas with a simple tense form, we have a phrase structure as in (51b). Now, the clitic is inside one of the conjuncts and so we expect this sentence to be bad because the subcategorization requirements of the verb in the righthand conjunct have been violated.

(51) a.

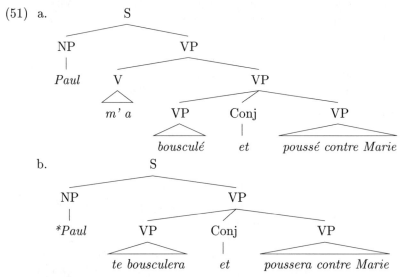

b.

3.4 Colloquial Italian and Crosslinguistic Concerns

The general theoretical point here is the LFG claim that there can be considerable, though not unlimited, independence between phrase structure configurations and relationships within the feature structure. The study of complex predicates provides further good evidence of this since we find that in identical phrase structure configurations, sometimes complex predicate formation occurs at the level of the feature structure and sometimes it does not. In other words, the issue of whether something is a complex predicate or not is not an issue of phrase structure. We illustrate this general point briefly with discussion of a construction in colloquial Italian and by reconsideration of the Urdu Permissive.

Rizzi (1982:35–36) mentions a special case of restructuring in colloquial Italian (which also appears in other varieties of Romance). One finds that the verb **sapere** 'know', which takes a CP complement, can sometimes form a complex predicate, as evidenced by clitic climbing, as in (52). The structure of (52b) is presumably roughly as in (53). Various details of this proposed structure are open to question, but unimportant. However, we take it as beyond question that **sapere** is here taking a full complement clause – a CP or its equivalent in other theories. On the other hand, note the clitic climbing which is definitive evidence of complex predicate formation.

(52) a. Su questo punto, non ti saprei che dire.
'On this point, I you wouldn't know what to tell.'
b. ?Mario, non lo saprei a chi affidare, durante le vacanze.
'Mario, I him wouldn't know to whom to entrust, during my holidays.'

(53)

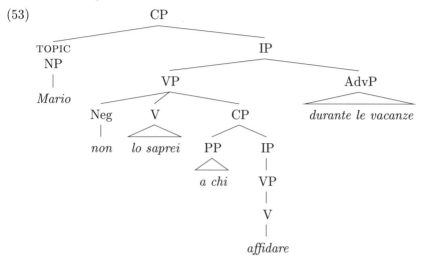

Such data have no natural explanation in the argument composition approach (if argument composition is taken to represent the surface phrase structure). Rather it suggests that complex predicate formation is a more abstract process that must be somewhat divorced from a particular phrase structure configuration. We want to be able to say that although such sentences preserve the same surface phrase structure as other instances of CP complementation, marginally the CP can cease to be a COMP at f-structure, but instead forms a complex predicate with the characteristic sharing of grammatical relations across the whole domain.

Stronger and more systematic evidence for the LFG separation of c-structure and f-structure can be found in other languages. A particularly good example is the evidence from Urdu that we discussed at the beginning of the last chapter, where phrase structural possibilities seem completely independent of whether complex predicate formation is occurring. Recall that there were two phrase structural possibilities – the 'complement' verb had to form a constituent with either its own object or with the main verb – but that these phrase structure possibilities occurred with both regular clausal complementation in the Instructive and complex predicate formation in the Permissive. While it is not impossible to combine the argument composition approach of HPSG with the existence of nested subordinate verb phrases (one simply has to allow partially saturated verb phrase constituents), such a move does not seem capable of explaining the verb agreement facts of Urdu within the framework of what is usually assumed for agreement in HPSG. Recall that in Urdu one had the Permissive complex predicate in (54a) with the phrase structure in (54b):

(54) a. Anjum ne   d-ii   Saddaf ko   [ciṭṭʰii
       Anjum ERG give-PERF.F.SG Saddaf DAT letter.F(NOM)
       likʰ-ne]
       write-INF
       'Anjum let Saddaf write a letter.'

   b.

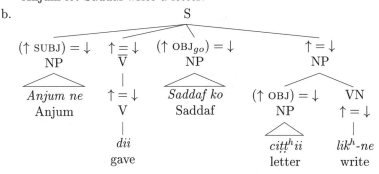

Under an argument composition account, **likʰ-ne** would take **ciṭṭʰii** as a regular complement, and then argument composition would occur with **d-ii** inheriting any remaining complements of the heavy verb (here there are none – the subject of **likʰ-ne** is not separately realized but simply coindexed with an argument of **d-ii**). The problem lurking here is that nowhere in this analysis is **ciṭṭʰii** an argument of **d-ii**. It is an argument of **likʰ-ne**, but it is removed from the COMPS list of **likʰ-ne** when the infinitival 'NP' is formed, before argument composition occurs. Therefore, there is no way for the light verb **d-ii** to get its hands on **ciṭṭʰii** so that it can agree with it, and yet agreement between this 'lower object' and the light verb is exactly what we find. Under the terms in which agreement is normally discussed in HPSG, this datum is thus a violation of Keenan's Principle: a verb is agreeing with something that is not one of its arguments. This is not a problem in our LFG account, however, since the light verb is agreeing with the least oblique nominative grammatical relation within the monoclausal array of grammatical relations resulting from complex predicate formation, just as always happens in Hindi/Urdu. This indicates the subtle but important difference between our conception and the argument composition view prevalent in current HPSG: under our conception, grammatical relations are genuinely shared across a domain of complex predicate formation, whereas under the argument composition approach it is only the case that (certain or all) complements are inherited upwards within the complex predicate.

Data such as the Italian and Urdu constructions we have just examined argue for the independence of phrase structure from functional structure that LFG has long advocated. One response to these data is to take a linearization-based approach within HPSG that abstracts surface word order and surface phrase groupings from underlying valence structure (e.g., Kathol 1995). In essence, this would mean that the arguments above simply show that French periphrastic tenses have a flat (i.e., monoclausal) grammatical relations structure, an analysis with which we agree. However, we take A&G to be making claims about surface phrase structure, and then the remarks of this section stand.

4 Conclusion

We have seen that the notion of sharing of TERMS lists gives a concrete and successful implementation of the idea that light verbs in some sense behave as auxiliaries, and such success is not possible without some concept of differential spreading. In particular, bidirectional sharing seems to have some advantages over the one directional inheritance that has been used in HPSG. Additionally, our careful account of feature classes allows us to deal correctly with verbal form, prepositional marking, auxiliary selection, and other features which often get passed over in big picture analyses of the phenomena.

Moving back to the arena of general linguistic theory, what we hope to have achieved is a method of handling the Romance data through use of a few clean and general formal ideas, rather than using ad-hoc devices which are specific to Romance. As a result of this, it is possible to extend our proposal beyond the domain of data that has previously been given a semi-formal treatment within the LFG complex predicates literature. To demonstrate this, and to provide some additional motivation for our approach, we will now look at the behavior of some serial verb constructions. Tariana (North Arawak) will be shown to be very similar to Romance at the feature structure level, even though very different in terms of phrase structure, while the Misumalpan languages of Nicaragua show not only different phrase structure patterns, but also very different patterns of information spreading within the feature structure. Nevertheless, despite these differences, they can both be given insightful formal analyses within the framework which we have proposed.

4

Serial Verb Constructions

In this chapter we will examine two so-called 'serial verb constructions' (SVCs), the first from the South American language Tariana, the second from the Central American language Miskitu. Although both of these constructions have been called SVCs by the people describing them, we will see that they are quite different from each other, and also quite different from various other constructions that have been called SVCs (see Lefebvre (1991) for a collection of studies).

After showing how our conception of information spreading provides straightforward analyses of both of these constructions, we will consider the question of whether 'Serial Verb Constructions' have any unifying characteristics, and, if so, what these might be. This will include brief discussion of other analyses of serial verbs such as Baker (1989) and Durie (1997).

It will be clear that these analyses of SVC constructions are far more tentative than those offered for the much-better studied Romance languages, since many fewer people have worked on these languages, and many important aspects of their structure remain unclear. But nonetheless, we believe that these analyses show that the framework presented in this monograph provides a promising basis for treating such constructions in a formal syntactic theory.

1   Serial verbs in Tariana

In this section we examine some of the serial verb constructions in Tariana, a North Arawakan language spoken in the Vaupés region of the Brazilian Amazon, based on the field work and initial analyses of Alexandra Aikhenvald.[1] Some general information about the language can be found in Aikhenvald (1994, to appear b) and a full grammar is in preparation.

---

[1] There are about 100 speakers, all bilingual in one of the various East Tucanoan languages, the dominant ones in the region. The language is obsolescent, not being learned by children. We are greatly indebted to Alexandra Aikhenvald for answering floods of queries, and providing us with paper drafts and manuscripts.

Aikhenvald (1995) provides a survey of SVC constructions and their relationship to other multi-verb constructions in the language. Two typical examples of SVCs in Tariana are the following:

(1) a. na-musu   na-nu   nema   diha-pua=nuku
       3PL-go out 3PL-come 3PL.stand he-CL:RIVER=TOPIC
       'They [the ancestors of the Tarianas] were coming out towards
       this [river].' (lit. go out - come - stand)

    b. nhaRitu na-inu=pidana   ñaña
       3PL.fish 3PL-kill=REMPAST:INFR madi
       'They caught [fished-killed] madi fish.'

Note the sequences of finite verbs, some of which apparently have a reduced meaning, giving a complex description of what speakers view as a single event.

1.1 Basic clause structure and SVCs

Tariana has variable word-order, with a tendency for the subject to be initial and the verb to be final. The grammar is clearly nominative-accusative in its overall organization, as indicated by both case-marking and agreement. Animate pronouns have a distinction between a bare nominative form, used in A and S function, and a marked form (which we will gloss OBL for oblique case) which marks pronouns serving in both syntactic O function, and in certain oblique functions.[2] Inanimates lack the oblique form, the nominative form being used for all of these functions. Secondly, there is a 'topic-marking' enclitic =**nuku** that can only be attached to nonsubjects. See Aikhenvald (1994) for further discussion of case-marking in general and the use of =**nuku** in particular. NPs can be freely omitted if their reference is recoverable from context, although pronouns seem to occur fairly often. Agreement comprises person/number (PN) prefixes that are normally found on 'active' verbs, but not on 'statives'. There is, however, one group of active verbs that do not show agreement, namely loan-verbs from Portuguese. Moreover, it is not clear exactly what determines the boundary between 'active' and 'stative'; **keru** 'be angry' is stative, while **kwisa** 'hate' and **yãmi** 'die, faint' are active:[3]

---

[2] A, S, and O are used in the sense of Andrews (1985) or Dixon (1994): A and O are the agent- and patient-like arguments of a transitive verb, while S is the single core argument of an intransitive verb. We note that at present it is often difficult to assess whether a given nonsubject NP is a term or an oblique, because there are only two processes that involve O, a passive and a reciprocalizing suffix, which are not yet well-enough understood for firm conclusions to be drawn.

[3] Tariana has a rather large number of enclitic particles expressing somewhat unfamiliar categories. In the glosses, these clitics are set off with an equals sign (=), semantic or grammatical components that do not get expressed as separate morphemes will be separated by colons, while glosses for morphemes that have undergone some fusion will be separated by periods. Some of the major categories of clitic particles are:

(2) a. nuha   keru=mha
      I.NOM angry=PRES:NONVIS
      'I am angry.'

    b. na-yãmi
      3PL-die/faint
      'They fainted/died.'[4]

    c. naha   na-kwisa wa-na
      they.NOM 3PL-hate 1PL-OBL
      'They hate us.'

Active verbs differ further from statives in that actives can occur in a wide range of serial verb constructions, while the occurrence of statives in SVCs is quite restricted.

One can argue that the essential characteristic of the active verbs is not possession of agreement *per se*, but rather that they have a morphological prefix position that needs to be filled by something, the agreement prefixes being the commonest option. The next most common option is a negative marker. Negation is expressed with a combination of a prefix **ma-** and a suffix **-(ka-)de**. But the prefix only appears with verbs that normally take an agreement prefix, and replaces that prefix as shown in (3) (examples of negated stative verbs without the prefix will appear below).

(3) **ma-**na-**kade**   du-yana   kuphe: Rafaeli-siu
    NEG-want-NEG 3SGF-cook fish   Rafael.POSS-for
    'She does not want to cook fish for Rafael.'

This suggests that statives and other verbs that lack an agreement prefix (such as Portuguese loan words) simply lack a morphological property that licenses the appearance of a prefix. In addition to the negative and the standard person/number agreements, there are two more agreement markers that occur in the prefix slot, an 'impersonal' marker **pa-**, whose use will be discussed below, and a relative marker **ka-**, used when the subject is the relativized-on NP in a relative clause, and also in a rather complex passive construction, discussed in Aikhenvald (to appear b).

Tariana SVCs are sequences of verbs which express a single semantic event. Each verb is a separate phonological word with its own stress and the ability to host clitics. The verbs each carry a concordant PN-prefix

---

Tense: PRES, RECPAST (recent past), REMPAST (Remote Past).
Evidentiality: VIS (Seen), NONVIS (not seen, perhaps heard), INFR (Inferred), SECH (Secondhand; hearsay).
Aspect/Aktionsart: CMPLT (Completive), IMPERF (Imperfective), DUR (Durative).
Other: DEP (Dependent), APPR (Approximative 'a little bit'), AFFECT (Affectedness), FRUSTR (Frustrative), REP (Repetitive 'again').

[4]This verb normally occurs in serialization with **-a** 'go': **na-yãmi na**. When 'go' is omitted, it is more likely to mean 'faint' than 'die'.

(except if the verb is stative), and the verbs of the SVC all share the same tense, aspect, mood, and evidentiality. These features are expressed by tense/aspect/mood/evidentiality (TAME) enclitic particles, which usually attach to one of the verbs, but can attach to any focussed constituent of the sentence. An SVC also allows only one negation, which scopes over the whole SVC. The verbs in an SVC are contiguous. They can be separated by enclitic TAME particles, and also by certain Aktionsart clitic particles, but not by NP arguments or adjuncts. Here are some more examples:

(4) a. i-na=mha   ye-me   hi=nuku
    2PL-want=PRES:NONVIS 2PL-sniff DEM:AN=TOPIC
    'You want to sniff this (snuff).'

    b. tarada-peni wa   wama=daka
       alive-PL:AN 1PL.go 1PL.look for=YET
       'We shall look for [go to-look-for] the live ones (fish) yet.'

In (4a) we see the object after the verb, bearing the =**nuku** marker, with the two components of the serial verb each bearing PN-marking, but separated by a (present, nonvisible) TAME clitic. (4b) is similar, except that the object appears in front of the serial verb.

SVCs can therefore plausibly be described as V-over-multiple-V constructions, fitting the following phrase-structure schema:

(5) V   →   V*

This form still allows the verbs in an SVC to be separated by material, such as TAME particles, which can plausibly be regarded as adjoined to V as a clitic. For example the verb in (4a) would get this structure:

(6)

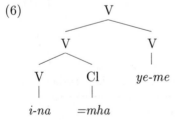

But this schema will exclude from appearing within an SVC material that cannot be regarded as adjoined to V, such as NP arguments. Current proposals about X-bar theory will in fact exclude the possibility of NP-nodes being introduced as daughters of V, so that the non-interruptability of these sequences may to some degree at least be explained rather than stipulated.

SVCs contrast with full-root verb-compounding constructions whose components do not behave like genuine standalone verbs, and with complement constructions, such as periphrastic causatives, where each verb seems to function as head of its own clause. The words in bold in (7) illustrate full-root verb-compounding of two stative verbs, here then joined in an SVC with an aspectual light verb (shown by square brackets). In full-root verb-compounding, the components cannot be separated by any clitics or suffixes, and the compound takes a single stress.

(7) naha pedaRia-pe [**matšia-puhwi-ka** na-wa=pidana]
    they old-PL   good-happy-DECL 3PL-enter=REMPAST:INFR
    'The old people became really happy.'

Observe that the TAME marker comes after the compound; if the sequence of stative verb-roots were an SVC, this would be surprising, because after the first V in an SVC seems to be a popular site for clitic particles to appear, while after the second is not.

In a complement construction, the verbs can carry independent marking for tense/evidentiality, aspect, etc., can show subject-agreement with different NPs, and the subordinate verb can take a dependency marker. Different PN marking and a dependency marker (**-ka**) are shown in the following periphrastic causative example:[5]

(8) nu-na   [ma:tči nu-Rena-ka=mha]   i-ni=yha
    1SG-OBL bad   1SG-feel=DEP-PRES:NONVIS 2PL-do=APPR
    'You made me feel miserable a little bit.'

SVCs further differ from complement structures and sequenced or coordinate clauses in terms of intonational properties. An SVC counts as a single prosodic phrase with one phrase accent (like a monoverbal clause), whereas complement structures and coordinations count as multiple prosodic phrases, which can be further demonstrated by the ability to separate them with a nasal pause marker.[6]

The phrase-structure configuration (5) serves as the basis for a considerable variety of clearly distinct types of SVC constructions, most of which are in fact binary, although there are substantial possibilities for combining different types with each other to yield longer constructions (the largest observed so far contains seven verbs).

---

[5]See Aikhenvald (to appear b) for discussion of the use of periphrastic vs. other kinds of causative constructions, with which Tariana is quite well-endowed.

[6]As Aikhenvald (1995) discusses, the verbs of sequenced and subordinate clauses may be followed by the nasal pause marker =**hã**, as in (i), but serial verbs cannot be separated in this way, so it would not be possible to put a pause marker after the second **na-nu** in (i).

(i) ne-sina   na-nu=hã,   [na-nu
    then-REMPAST:NONVIS 3PL-come=PAUSE 3PL-come
    nema=sina=hã]
    3PL.stand=REMPAST:NONVIS=PAUSE
    'Then they [Tarianas] came, they were coming.'

Aikhenvald classifies these into three fundamental types, symmetric, asymmetric and ambient, with various further divisions of these categories. Symmetric and ambient serializations are composed of open-class items, and we will discuss these first, proposing an analysis for the symmetrics but not the ambients. Asymmetric serializations on the other hand consist of an open class item plus a closed one. They are therefore reminiscent of light-verb constructions, and we will analyse them accordingly.

1.2 Symmetric and ambient SVCs

Symmetric SVCs are sequences of open-class verbs which agree in transitivity. They are thus similar to the cases of SVCs analysed by Bodomo (1996). The verbs are all equivalent in headship properties for the construction; none could be strongly argued to take the others as complements, for example. Ambient serializations on the other hand involve two open class items, one of which seems to function in some kind of adverbial relationship.

Some sample symmetric SVC constructions are shown in (9).

(9) a. ma [wa-wa   wa-dana] wa-yarupe=nuku
       let's 1PL-read/play 1PL-write 1PL-thing=TOPIC
       'Let's read and write up our language!'

   b. phia=nihka   [phita   pi-thake-ta
      you=PAST:VIS 2SG.take 2SG-cross.CAUS-AFFECT
      pi-eme]   ha-ne-na   hyapa-na-nuku?
      2SG-stand.CAUS DEM-DIST-CL:VERT hill-CL:VERT-TOPIC
      'Was it you who brought that mountain across?'
      (lit. take - cross - put upright)

   c. na-ira=sita=pidana
      3PL-drink=AFTER:SS=REMPAST:INFR
      [[na-inu-kaka=pidana   na-ita]
      3PL-'kill'-RECIP=REMPAST:INFR 3PL-shoot arrow
      neyu]
      3PL.go upstream
      'After they had drunk, they fought each other with arrows and went upstream.'

Sentence (a) illustrates a binary, (b) a ternary branching SVC, while (c) will be argued below to involve one binary symmetric structure nested inside another. In (b), the requirement that symmetric serial verbs have the same core arguments has led to the second and third verbs being morphologically causativized. The morpheme **ta** glossed 'AFFECT' is a further formative that often appears on causatives, which is here used to emphasize the effect on the Patient, not to form a genuine double causative. In (c), the second verb consists of a transitive stem followed by a reciprocalizing suffix, creating a derived intransitive, so that all the verbs again agree in transitivity.

The components of a symmetric serialization seem to refer to temporally distinct phases of an event, presented linearly in an iconic order, whereas for example in ambient serializations the verbs refer to simultaneously existing or intrinsically unorderable phases (as for example the posture assumed by the agent during the performance). When reference is to an activity occupying an indefinite expanse of time, these phases are randomly interleaved, as in (a), while when the reference is to a single event, the phases are ordered iconically, as in (b). Example (c) can be regarded as a combination of both possibilities: **na-inu-kaka=pidana na-ita** 'fight-each-other shoot-arrows' would appear to be a 2-part symmetric causative referring to interleaved activities that take place over a period of time, and then this period is treated as an event and then serialized with **neyu** 'go upstream'. This can be informally indicated by the following diagram:

(10)

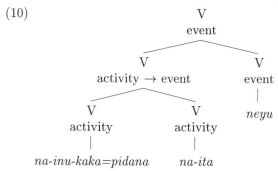

Note that the discourse-particle **pidana** is attached to the first member of the embedded symmetric SVC. This is another example of the capacity of clitics to interrupt constituents (indeed, such clitics commonly occur on the first member of an SVC).

The semantics of symmetric serialization seems to be very similar or perhaps even identical to that of non-boolean verb coordination in English.[7] A plausible syntactic basis for such interpretations would be provided if the components of a symmetric SVC each contributed an element to a set. From a strictly syntactic point of view the easiest thing to do would be to provide symmetric SVCs with a set-valued LCS. The set of grammatical relations ρ would on the other hand be shared by all verbs(so that the verbs will agree), while we can account for the transitivity agreement by sharing the TERMS attribute as well.[8] The following rule will achieve this:

---

[7] As pointed out to us by Henriette de Swart.

[8] It is not possible to attribute the transitivity sharing constraint to the sharing of grammatical relations, since verbs can share grammatical relations without sharing transitivity, as in the asymmetric causative serializations that we consider later in the chapter.

(11) V $\quad\rightarrow\quad$ V*

$\qquad\qquad={\{\text{TERMS},\rho\}}$

$\qquad\qquad(\uparrow \text{LCS}) \in (\downarrow \text{LCS})$

As before, this rule can be viewed as somewhat informal, in that the phrase structure categories express that the category and bar level projections, κ and β, are also shared between all nodes in the above rule. And again, note how this is a form of complex predicate formation that cannot be licensed under the proposals of Alsina (1997), since each verb is a semantically complete predicate.

The verb in (9a) will then get the following structure:

(12)

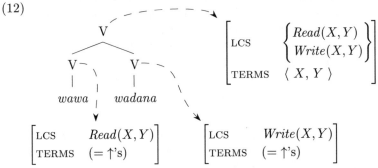

(some arrows replaced by informal references to reduce clutter)

The formulation of (11) unifies the TERMS attributes of the members of the SVC in order to produce one for the entire construction. The independent manipulation of the TERMS and LCS attributes allows a straightforward analysis of the transitivity agreement between the members of the SVC, while allowing composition of the LCS values into a set value.

But there is a good possibility that this merger can be dispensed with. The appearance of agreement on each verb in the SVC indicates that at least one member of ρ, SUBJ, is shared. If it is the entire ρ projection that is shared (as asserted by (11)), then it becomes possible that the TERMS-list of each component verb is independently linked with the grammatical relations:

(13)

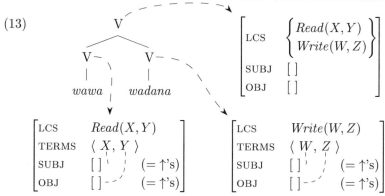

(some arrows replaced by informal references to reduce clutter)

The viability of this idea depends on the details of how linking theory works, and how the principles of Completeness and Coherence are implemented: it will work if Completeness and Coherence are assessed individually for each member V in the SVC. We will discuss some of the relevant issues in Appendix B, where we discuss glue-language semantics.

Ambient serialization differs from symmetric in that there is no requirement for transitivity agreement: one of the verbs is intransitive, having some kind of adverbial or other modificatory relationship to the other verb:

(14) a. diha diha hipatu hiku-pana   ma-kade=pidana
        he   he   snuff appear-ALL NEG.give-NEG=REMPAST:INFR
        'He (the traditional God) did not give (her) the stuff in a totally visible way (lit. appear-give).'

  b. thuya ha-ehkwapeni=nuku   nawiki=nuku di-kaRite
        all   DEM-world+PL:AN=TOPIC people=TOPIC 3SGNF-tell
        di-peya-ka=pidana
        3SGNF-be first-DECL=REMPAST:INFR
        'He was the first to tell (lit. tell-be first) all the people in the world (about the discovery of fire).'

In the (a) example the usual PN-marking does not appear, being missing from the first V because it is stative, and from the second because it is negative: the negative prefix **ma-** pre-empts the PN-marker. In (b) on the other hand, the verbs are non-stative and positive, so the PN-markers appear as usual.

A further difference between ambient and symmetric serialization is that the verbs seem to refer to simultaneously existing aspects of a situation, rather than to temporally distinct phases of an event or activity, as is the case with symmetric ones. We will not make a specific proposal for the analysis of ambient serialization, but it is probably correct to regard one verb as a light verb, as in asymmetric serializations, only that with ambient serializations, the light verb is drawn from an open class. This is reflected in the fact that the verbs in an ambient serialization are not required to share transitivity, and the modifying daughter of the SVC cannot itself have recursive structure, just as in asymmetric serializations.

1.3 Asymmetric serialization

The final type, asymmetric, falls into quite a number of subcategories; here we will briefly discuss modal, causative, aspectual, and motion serializations, ignoring associatives.[9] Modal SVCs have as their first and 'light' element one of the verbs **-na** 'want', **-uma** 'strive for, look for', **-a** 'be going to (FUT)', and **ira** 'need'.[10] The heavy element comes second, and is interpreted in the same general manner as a complement. We have already seen some examples of this kind in (4). Modal SVCs are binary, presumably because of their semantic interpretation.

Similar to the modals in form are causative SVCs. Here the light element is one of the verbs **a** 'go, give, get to, say' (for plain causatives), **wana** 'call', **matara** 'give permission to, leave', or **ira** 'order', and again comes before the heavy element. We describe these as 'causatives' because the Agent of the light verb is allowing, causing or encouraging the occurrence of the event described by the heavy verb. The causee take oblique case if an animate pronominal (18) or the non-subject topic **=nuku** marker, as in (15b):

(15) a. ka:ru-ka   nuha nu-a=mahka   nu-hyã=niki
        fear-DECL I   1SG-give=RECPAST:NONVIS 1SG-eat=COMPLT
        piri=nuku   di-a=pidana
        2SG.son=TOPIC 3SGNF-say-REMPAST:INFR
        'Being afraid, I let (the fish) eat your son, he said.'

    b. nu-inipe=nuku   kwaka-mhade nu-a   nu-hña
        1SG-children=TOPIC how-FUT   1SG-let 1SG-eat
        'How will I get my children to eat [if I can't hunt anything]?'

In (a) we start out with a circumstantial adjunct **ka:ruka** 'being afraid', then we have a nominative subject pronoun (the nonsubject form would be **nu-na**), and finally our causative SVC. The first component (Cause) V is unremarkable (the gloss 'NONVIS' indicates that the event was not seen happening), but the second (Effect) V is rather surprising, because it shows subject agreement with the putative matrix subject, which is not even one

---

[9] For some information about these, see (Aikhenvald to appear a).

[10] The last differs from the others in not taking a PN-marker, as indicated by the absence of the initial dash, and is furthermore involved in an interesting agreement phenomenon, as will be discussed further below.

of its own participants. This same agreement phenomenon occurs in (b), and will receive considerable attention below.

A causative serialization can be the heavy component of a modal serialization (still with concordant subject inflection!):

(16) a. [hekuda=nuku pi-na-ka   pi-a   pi-hỹa nun-na]
        [fruit=TOPIC 2SG-want-DEP 2SG-let 2SG-eat 1SG-OBL]
        pi-sepata pini=tha=sika   phia
        2SG-suffer 2SG-do-FRUSTR=PRES:INFR you
        'Wishing to let me eat the fruit, you suffered.'

     b. nu-na=tha   nu-ra   nu-sata dineiru
        1SG-want=FRUSTR 1SG-order 1SG-ask money
        'I want to order (him) to ask for money.'

The first example is from a traditional story, the second elicited; in both, the order is what would be expected from embedding if, in modal serialization, the light component comes first and the heavy second. Other orders do not seem to be possible here, and a modal serialization cannot be embedded inside a causative (perhaps for semantic reasons).

The next type is aspectual serialization. Here the light component is one of a number of motion, posture or phase (e.g. 'start' or 'finish') verbs, but unlike with modal serialization, it normally comes second:

(17) tuiri-kere   na-hwa   nema
     bird-island 3PL-stay 3PL.stand
     'They stayed at Bird Island for a long time.'

Aspectual serialization can combine ambiguously with causative serialization:

(18) na-na   dura   du-pita   du-yã=nhi
     3PL-OBL 3SGF.order 3SGF-bathe 3SGF-stay=DUR
     'She used to order them to bathe.' or
     'She ordered them to usually bathe.'

This ambiguity is consistent with the phrase-structural possibilities: since the aspectual comes after the heavy verb it combines with, it can be seen as applying to either the entire complex **dura du-pita** to produce the first meaning, or **du-pita** alone to produce the second:

(19) a.

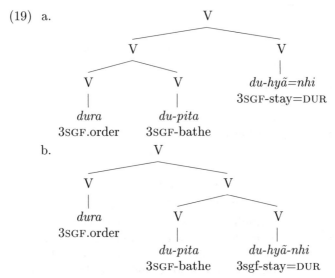

However, it is apparently not possible for an aspectual verb to appear between the Cause and Effect verbs in a sequence of three verbs like this.

Motional serialization also has the light component second. The light component is furthermore frequently although not always a two-component element, the first describing the motion with respect to intrinsic features of the situation, the second orienting it with respect to a narrative point of view:

(20) ... nha ke:ča   na-doReta nhe   na=pidana
     ... they black ants 3PL-carry 3PL.enter 3PL.go=REMPAST:INFR
     na-ya-yawa-se
     3PL-POSS-CL:HOLE-LOC
     '[after the young man gave them some manioc flour], the black ants carried it away into their hole.'

In this SVC, the second verb, the first motion verb, characterizes the motion of going into something, the ants' hole, while the second describes it as going away from the narrative point of view, the position of a young man who is engaging in negotiations with the ants. Even when not serialized with another activity verb, motion verbs tend to occur in pairs, in this way:[11]

(21) na-mara   na-nu=sina=pita
     3PL-go down 3PL-come=REMPAST:NONVIS=REP
     'They came down again.'

Therefore it would seem plausible to think of these motion serializations as

---

[11] See also (1a) for another example then further serialized with an aspectual verb.

inherently binary, with the motional component itself tending to be binary, although this is not a requirement.

The analysis of these asymmetric SVC constructions, to which we turn below, will obviously be quite different from that of the symmetric SVCs, since their semantics is not at all like that of coordination, but like that of complementation, and light verbs in the Romance languages. Indeed, the classifications of aspectual, modal, motion, and causative serializations greatly overlap with the categories of light verbs in Romance, as identified, for instance, by Rizzi (1978) for Italian. On the other hand, the appearance of a variety of different abstract syntactic and semantic structures being associated with the one V-under-V phrase-structure format is highly compatible with the leading ideas of the LFG architecture. Moreover, we will see that the proposals of this monograph support a reasonably simple implementation.

1.4 Modal and causative SVCs as light verb constructions

In Classic LFG, there would be essentially two possible analyses for modal and causative SVCs. One would be to say that they were a strictly lexicon-internal structure with no ramifications for the syntax at all. In (4a), repeated below as (22), for example, the lexical items for 'want' and 'sniff' would be combined into a single lexical item meaning 'want to sniff', and the LFG syntax would be responsible for providing this complex with its arguments, but not for explaining any of its properties.

(22) i-na=mha   yeme   hi=nuku
    2PL-want=PRES:NONVIS 2PL.sniff DEM:AN=TOPIC
    'You want to sniff this (snuff).'

These assumptions would leave quite a lot of the grammar of Tariana outside of the scope of LFG. For modal serializations we do not now have any clear arguments that this is actually wrong, but for causative serializations there is one, which is that a time adverbial in the clause-structure can modify either the cause or the effect verb:

(23) na-na   du-ra=nhi   du-ita   depita
    3PL-OBL 3SGF-order=DUR 3SGF-bathe at night
    'She ordered them to bathe at night.'

Like its English translation, this sentence is ambiguous in whether the bathing or the ordering is being said to happen at night. Such ambiguity is not generally found with strictly lexical causativization: *He whitened the clothes at night* is not similarly ambiguous as to what time he acted vs. what time the clothes became white. This kind of ambiguity is however characteristic both of standard complement structures, and of the complex predicate structures that we have seen previously.

A purely lexical analysis does not therefore seem to be indicated. Turning to syntactic possibilities, in Classic LFG the only plausible prospect would be to treat the heavy component as being the XCOMP of the light one. It would then be necessary to introduce the nonsubject arguments with functional uncertainty expressions such as ($\uparrow$ XCOMP* OBJ) and ($\uparrow$ XCOMP* ADJUNCT), in order to allow them to function as the object or adjunct of an XCOMP as well as a simple top-level OBJ or XCOMP.[12] On this analysis, (15b) would get an f-structure like this:

(24)

$$
\begin{bmatrix}
\text{SUBJ} & \begin{bmatrix} \text{PRED} & \text{'Pro'} \\ \text{NUM} & \text{PL} \\ \text{PERS} & \text{III} \end{bmatrix} \\
\text{PRED} & \text{'Order}\langle \text{SUBJ, OBJ, XCOMP} \rangle \\
\text{OBJ} & \begin{bmatrix} \text{PRED} & \text{'Pro} \\ \text{NUM} & \text{SG} \\ \text{PERS} & \text{III} \end{bmatrix} \\
\text{XCOMP} & \begin{bmatrix} \text{SUBJ} & [\ ] \\ \text{PRED} & \text{'Stop}\langle \text{SUBJ, OBJ} \rangle \text{'} \\ \text{OBJ} & \begin{bmatrix} \text{PRED} & \text{'Pro'} \end{bmatrix} \end{bmatrix}
\end{bmatrix}
$$

But it should be clear that this kind of structure provides no account at all of the most striking feature of the construction, the appearance on the Effect verb of a subject-marker agreeing with the Causer. Since, on this analysis, it is the Causee rather than the Causer that is the SUBJ of the Effect verb, it is the Causee, if anything, that we expect to find the Effect verb agreeing with. In particular, the observed agreement behavior contrasts with that of subordinating periphrastic causatives, which also occur in Tariana. In periphrastic causatives, like (25) (or (8)), each verb does agree with its own subject. Moreover, in this construction, the causative verb usually occurs after the subordinate clause, the dependency marker **-ka** is possible or required on the subordinate verb, and one can observe the contrasts observed earlier between complex clauses and SVCs. For instance, one can insert a pausal marker, or one can place negation or TAME particles separately on each verb, as in (8). For the periphrastic causative, an ordinary XCOMP analysis seems quite appropriate (and it does not require functional uncertainty in GF assignment).

(25) diha emi-peni=nuku   nema-ka   di-ni=ka
     he   child-PL:AN=TOPIC 3PL.sleep-DEP 3SGNF-do=RECPAST:VIS
     'He made the children sleep (with a special effort).'

---

[12]See Matsumoto (1995) for such an analysis of Japanese.

But the properties of the causative SVC are quite consistent with those of the complex predicate structures we have been considering earlier. We have observed that sharing of grammatical relations across the various levels of a causative construction is a widespread and long-known phenomenon, and have proposed to analyse it in Romance and various other kinds of languages in terms of a grammatical attribute ARG that the standard grammatical relations SUBJ, OBJ and ADJUNCT spread across.

Suppose that the schema for causative serializations in Tariana is:

$$(26) \quad V \quad \rightarrow \quad \underset{\substack{=\{\rho,\alpha\}}}{V} \quad \underset{\substack{=\{\rho\} \\ \text{ARG}}}{V}$$

The feature-structure specified by the lexical entry for a causative serializing verb can then be almost identical to that for a 3-place causative light verb in Romance:

$$(27) \begin{bmatrix} \text{LCS} & Cause(X,Y,Z) \\ \text{TERMS} & \langle X, \underbrace{Y \mid \ldots}\rangle \\ \\ \text{ARG} & \begin{bmatrix} \text{TERMS} & \langle \ldots \rangle \\ \text{LCS} & Z \end{bmatrix} \end{bmatrix}$$

Here, the relationship between the TERMS-lists of the two verbs is again given by (↑ TERMS REST) = (↑ ARG TERMS). The only feature-structural difference between this structure and that of a Romance verb is that here no form features are imposed on the pseudo-complement ARG-value. Thus differences are confined to a different phrase structure and a very superficial morphological difference. And just as with the Romance structure, the heavy verb's LCS will be appropriately unified with the light verb's, without involvement of a complement structure.

The SUBJ-sharing immediately accounts for the 'concordant dependent' agreement in the causative constructions, and also for the adverbial ambiguities, in the same way as proposed in other languages where we have adopted this form of analysis. On the other hand, our treatment of the Effect verb's syntactic arguments is speculative: we have simply followed the model of Romance languages, without having clear evidence as to whether the Effect Agent and Patient are really terms, or are instead obliques, as is typologically possible. There are two known constructions that might in principle assist in investigating this issue, passives, and the reciprocal/detransitivizing suffix -kaka (already encountered in (9c)). Unfortunately, the passive can be based only on simple verbs, not SVCs (it is itself a rather complex construction involving serialization), and it is not known what the results are of trying to apply -kaka to a causative light verb.

This analysis entails that when a two-place verb is causativized via an SVC a three-place predicate results. We should then expect, and indeed do find, that there are three-place predicates in the language that express both their non-subject arguments as bare non-nominative NPs. Compare (16a) with (28) below (Aikhenvald, p.c., 1997):

(28) kana nu-a=mahka   na-na
      corn 1SG-give=RECPAST:NONVIS they-OBL
      'I gave them corn.'

Modal and aspectual serializations submit easily to the same kind of treatment, except with simpler TERMS composition. For a modal serialization such as (22), we can use the same c-structural form as for causatives, but with a structure like (29a) for the modal light verb. This means that the whole SVC will have the feature structure outlined in (29b).

(29) a.
$$\begin{bmatrix} \text{LCS} & [\mathit{Want}(X,Y)] \\ \text{TERMS} & \langle \underbrace{X, \ldots}\rangle \\ & \\ \text{ARG} & \begin{bmatrix} \text{TERMS} & \langle \ldots \rangle \\ \text{LCS} & Y \end{bmatrix} \end{bmatrix}$$

    b.
$$\begin{bmatrix} \text{LCS} & [\mathit{Want}(X, \underbrace{\mathit{Sniff}(X,Z)}_{Y})] \\ \text{TERMS} & \langle \underbrace{X, Z}\rangle \\ & \\ \text{ARG} & \begin{bmatrix} \text{TERMS} & \langle \ldots \rangle \\ \text{LCS} & Y \end{bmatrix} \end{bmatrix}$$

Here the upper and lower terms lists are simply identified. In an equational notation, this can be indicated snappily as simply (↑ TERMS) = (↑ ARG TERMS). The 'want' verb ascribes a semantic role to the top TERM, but does not introduce any new ones. This is again the same feature-structural analysis as we have proposed for Romance (and is basically what was proposed by Rosen (1989)).

A further piece of evidence which give some additional support for this analysis is the formation of subject relative clauses, where the normal PN agreement marker is replaced by **ka-**. This happens on all verbs of a serialization:

(30) diha iñe   di-thi-sedite   naha nawiki **kema**
     he   devil 3SGNF-eye-WITHOUT.CL:AN they people REL.stand
     ka-kwa=nuku   puaya=pidana   di-ni=pita
     REL-hang=TOPIC different=REMPAST:INFR 3SGNF-do-REP
     'The eyeless devil did something else to the people who were
     hanging (in the hammocks).'

Again, the appearance of the relativization marker on the subordinate verb
makes little sense if there were an XCOMP here, but is expected and explained under the hypothesis that the TERMS lists are shared.

On grounds of the desirability of restrictiveness in linguistic theory,
one might think that because of the substantial morphological and c-
structural differences between them, it is undesirable to give virtually identical feature-structures to light verbs in Romance and asymmetric SVCs in
Tariana. But the discussion of Urdu in Chapter 2 shows that there is in fact
a high degree of independence between c-structure and feature-structure:
in Urdu, both light verbs and XCOMP constructions can each be associated
with either a NP over VP complement or a V – V form of c-structure.
What we see in Tariana is just another instance of this kind of freedom.

Further corroboration for our analysis comes from the agreement properties of the modal serializing verb **ira** 'need', which belongs to a small class
of stative verbs (referring to physical states) that takes its sole argument
in the oblique rather than the nominative case:[13]

(31) dai=mha   nu-na
     sleep=PRES:NONVIS 1SG-OBL
     'I am sleepy.'

In modal serializations with **ira** 'need', the 'Needer' role is expressed by
an oblique, while the heavy component takes the impersonal agreement-
marker **pa-**:

(32) nu-na   ira-mha   pa-ni   patsi yaphini ha
     1SG-OBL need=PRES:NONVIS IMPERS-do other thing   DEM:INAN
     ehkwapi-ne
     world-INS
     'It is necessary for me to make other things in the world.'

This is hard to account for on the XCOMP analysis, because this analysis
would say that the 'Needer' is the SUBJ of the lower verb, but would gen-
erate no expectation that the lower verb could not agree with the Needer
in person and number in the normal manner.

This is because the lexical entries and morphology for active verbs motivated by the basic data of the language will have forms specifying the PERS

---

[13]These verbs appear to have some interesting properties with respect to serialization
that we will not investigate here.

and NUM attributes for the SUBJ of the verb. In the 'need' construction, this SUBJ-value happens to carry a non-nominative case-specification, but there is nothing elsewhere in the data that shows that this should block agreement, which is therefore expected.[14] The argument-structure-based complex predicate treatment on the other hand supports a straightforward account. Suppose that the oblique arguments of these verbs are not bearers of SUBJ, but rather of OBJ (or perhaps OBL), and that the predicates themselves are either subjectless, or have only a 'silent dummy' SUBJ-value. The feature-structure determined by the lexical entry for **ira** 'need' will then be:

(33) *ira*:
$$\begin{bmatrix} \text{LCS} & Need(X,Y) \\ \text{TERMS} & \langle X \mid \ldots \rangle \text{-----} \\ \text{OBJ} & \text{---} \\ \text{ARG} & \begin{bmatrix} \text{LCS} & Y \\ \text{TERMS} & \langle \ldots \rangle \text{--} \end{bmatrix} \end{bmatrix}$$

The line connecting the first position on the top-level TERMS-list with the value of OBJ indicates that this argument is realized as an OBJ, while the line connecting the two TERMS-values indicates that these are to be identified.

As a result, the top term of the lower verb is realized as an OBJ rather than as a SUBJ, and so will not provide person and number features for the agreement morphology, which appears to be sensitive to grammatical relations rather than semantic roles (as independently evidenced by the agreement in causatives).

But what then of the 'impersonal' agreement **pa-**? This is normally used when the subject is 'indefinite', similar to French **on** or German **man**, or the 'autonomous' verbal inflection in Irish:

(34) ne-se=na   pha   pa-sape
    then-LOC=REMPAST:VIS IMPERS:PRONOUN IMPERS-talk
    pa-bueta   na-ine=nuku
    IMPERS-learn 3PL-INSTR=TOPIC
    'Then one learned to talk from/with them.'[15]

Since it lacks specific features of person and number, it would be a plausible form to use if **ira** and other 'sole oblique argument' predicates are either fully subjectless in their syntax, or take some kind of 'silent dummy' or pro argument as their subject.

---

[14] As it is for example found with oblique-controlled XCOMPs in Icelandic (Andrews 1990:207-208).

[15] From a story about how people from different tribes were put together in one classroom and taught to speak just one language, Tucano, instead of several.

The failure of agreement to apply as usual with these forms is therefore predicted, and the prospects would seem good for fully explaining the choice of marker actually used, since the properties of the impersonal agreement marker are the nearest to being appropriate when no subject at all is present.

1.5   The μ-Projection

Of the many issues we have not addressed, one of the largest is the question of the treatment of the μ-projection in Tariana SVCs. Our intuitive expectation is that μ would be shared, and one might imagine that the shared PN-marking of the members of an SVC provides evidence of this, but this is actually not the case, because the shared PN-marking follows as a consequence of the sharing of SUBJ (subsumed under the sharing of ρ).

Many plausible candidates for membership in μ, such as tense, mood and evidentiality, are expressed as clitics that appear preferentially on the verb, but can be attached to any focussed constituent (Aikhenvald to appear b). Of the various formatives that attach specifically to verbs, only negation seems plausibly analysed as involving a μ-feature. But negation is not marked on all the members of the SVC, but only once, normally on the first verb. In a causative SVC, the semantic scope of a negation on the first verb, the causative light verb, can be either the whole causation or just the Effect verb. For example, in (35), the negated causative SVC could mean either 'he did not order them to kill many fish' or 'he ordered them not to kill many fish (but just a few)'. In the narrative context in which this example appears, it is clear that the latter reading was intended.

(35) hanupe-se   mara-kade=ka   dinu
      many-CONTRAST NEG.order=NEG=RECPAST:VIS 3SGNF.kill
      diha-yawa   i-minali   du-a=tha=pidana
      he-CL:HOLE INDF-master 3SGF-say=FRUSTR=REMPAST:INRF
      ' "The master of the (water)hole ordered not to kill many fish" said (the widow) in vain.'

Sharing of μ between the members of an SVC can explain how negation can be marked on the upper verb while being interpreted on the lower, but it does not explain why it is marked only once, on the first. The first verb is negated even in symmetric SVCs:

(36) a. ma-kalite-kade=pidana   du-pala
         NEG-tell-NEG=REMPAST:INFR 3SGF-put
         'She did not report, or tell, or complain.'

b. ihya-ne=naka   ma-dia-kade   i-yema
you-AG=PRES:VIS NEG-return-NEG 2PL-stand
i-yeka=naka   na   na-sape=naka
2PL-know=PRES:VIS 3PL.say 3PL-speak=PRES:VIS
'You will not know how to return, they are saying.'

A constraint that might account for this effect would be one to the effect that a negative marker must c-structurally precede all of the verbs that are within its semantic scope. This effect would then be reminiscent of negative polarity items such as *ever* and *any*. We will not develop such an account here, but if this is the appropriate approach, then it could be handled via an adaptation of the notion of functional precedence (Kaplan 1995).

The other specifically verbal affixes are Aktionsart particles, which seem to apply to whatever verb they modify, and various valence-altering and derivational formatives, such as nominalizers and relativizers. These all differ from the negative in that when they apply to a symmetric SVC, they appear at the end, so that their overt syntactic scope mirrors their apparent semantic scope. With asymmetric serialization on the other hand, they typically appear after the first element, which will be the light verb in the case of modal and causative SVCs, and the heavy verb for motional and directional SVCs. This seems consistent with these markers contributing material to the α-projection rather than ρ or μ, but considerably more extensive study will be required to yield a convincing analysis.

1.6 Upshot

While considerable work remains to be done to understand all aspects of Tariana SVCs, nevertheless Tariana clearly shows how the functional relationships expressed in many languages through morphological derivation or complex predicates formed from pseudo-complement-taking light verbs can also be realized as serial verb constructions involving combinations of V^0s. This argues against a strong distinction between serial verbs and other complex predicates (as suggested by Butt (1995:223–226), for example). We have in fact been able to show that the kind of separation of various sorts of information that we propose means that Tariana asymmetric SVCs can be given an analysis that is identical to that for Romance light verbs in all appropriate respects.

2 Misumalpan causatives

In this section we look at some SVC constructions in Miskitu, a Central American language spoken by several tens of thousands of people in Nicaragua and Honduras, recently discussed in (Salamanca 1988) and Hale

(1989, 1991).[16] Miskitu is traditionally regarded as a member of the 'Misumalpan' language family, together with Sumu and the extinct Matagalpan. Although this grouping has not been adequately justified by the comparative method, Miskitu and Sumu have been spoken together for a long time, and their syntax is very similar. They seem in particular to be almost identical in their serial verb constructions. Here we will for the most part restrict our attention to Miskitu, because it has more speakers and there is somewhat more information about it available.

In the following subsections we will begin by surveying complex sentence structures as presented by Salamanca (1988) and Hale (1991), and we will then focus on the causative serializations for which we will propose an analysis.

2.1 Types of Complex Sentences

On the basis of obvious facts of morphology and word-order, Miskitu complex sentences fall into two types: complement constructions and serialization constructions. The complement constructions seem to be entirely unremarkable, being highly reminiscent of complementation in Indo-European languages such as Spanish, except that heads are final ((Salamanca 1988:280):[17]

(37) a. Yang [Bilwi ra waia] want sna
     I   Bilwi to go.INF want be.PRES.1
     'I want to go to Bilwi.'

   b. Yang want sna   [Maria Bilwi ra wabia]
     I   want be.PRES.1 Maria Bilwi ra go.ABS.VRT.3
     'I want Maria to go to Bilwi.'

---

[16]We are greatly indebted here to Ken Hale, Maria Bittner, and Danilo Salamanca, and indirectly to their consultants and various co-workers, for discussion and data. Many of the examples below are from an undated data handout entitled 'Misumalpan Causative Data', collected by various people and compiled by Ken Hale, noted as 'MCD', and some is from a problem set 'Miskitu Causative Constructions', by Ken Hale (1989) (MCC). Other data is from (Bittner 1997), (Hale 1989) (CCM), (Hale 1991) (MVSQ), (Salamanca 1988) (ELM) or as otherwise indicated.

[17]Salamanca presents Miskitu verbs as expressing categories of Aspect, Tense, Mood, Polarity and subject person. Syntactically independent 'indicative' verbs have an aspectual distinction traditionally called 'absolute' vs. 'indefinite', whose meaning is not very clear to us, but where the 'indefinite' seems to be the unmarked form, the 'absolutive' a marked one indicating that the event is momentary or disconnected from the present situation. Forms without an ABS gloss will be 'indefinite'. The tenses are present, past and future, the persons 1, 2 and 3. The future forms have uses in subordinate clauses, where the future perfective is sometimes regarded as being a subjunctive, the imperfective a conditional. There are first and second person imperatives with a negative form for the latter. Finally there are syntactically dependent forms that can be seen as marking a proximate vs. obviative switch-reference system, as discussed below.

In (a) the complement verb is an infinitive with understood subject coreferential to the matrix subject; the complement could also be reordered to a position after the main verb. In (b) the subordinate verb is future perfective, often referred to as 'subjunctive' when subordinate. The main verb here consists of a borrowed nominal plus a form of the copula. A few verbs also take complements bearing the proximate/obviative morphology discussed below (Hale 1991:5–6).

The serial constructions on the other hand consist of a sequence of clauses whose verbs are in nonfinal forms without semantically autonomous tense, but marking a proximate/obviative distinction that we will discuss shortly, followed by a final clause whose verb is in a normal tense-marked form. The nonfinal verbs appear in what may be called 'proximate' forms when all the verbs in the sequence share the same subject, 'obviative' forms when they don't. This distinction is often described as an opposition between 'participial' and 'connexive' forms, presumably on the basis that the proximate/participials don't show person marking in Miskitu and Southern Sumu (Ulwa), but they do in Northern Sumu (Panamahka; (Norwood 1987), cited in (Hale 1991:14)). This suggests that the proximate/obviative terminology is in fact more appropriate than the participial/connexive. The nonfinal forms do however carry a redundant partial respecification of the tense on the final form (Hale 1991:14), in that the obviative has one set of forms (Virtual) when the final tense is future, another (Actual) when it isn't.[18] But this uniform morphological format is used for at least two very different kinds of grammatical construction.

First are what Salamanca calls 'chaining constructions', which might also be called 'consecutive clause constructions'. Here each clause in the series refers to a distinct, independent event, and perhaps apart from subject-sharing, behaves as an independent syntactic unit. These examples illustrate shared and different-subject clause-chaining:

(38) a. Pedro buk kum plik-i,   naha na sak-i,   Maria-ra
       Pedro book a   look for-PROX, this   find-PROX, Maria-to
       yab-an
       give-PAST.3
       'Pedro looked for a book, found it, and gave it to Maria.'
       (ELM:289)

---

[18] These forms are termed 'virtual' and 'actual' connexive by Salamanca (1988); we will gloss them as OBV:VRT and OBV:ACT respectively. The proximate (PROX) forms in Miskitu and Ulwa don't mark tense, although they do in Panamahkan.

    b. Pedro buk kum plik-ka,   naha na sak-ka,
       Pedro book a   look for-OBV:VRT.3, this   find-OBV:VRT.3,
       Maria-ra yabia.
       Maria-to give.ABS:FUT.3
       'When Pedro$_i$ looks for a book and (s)he$_j$ finds it, (s)he$_k$ will
       give it to Maria.' (ELM:289)

The other kind of construction shows a substantially greater degree of combination between the participant clauses, and appears to come in a number of subvarieties. The one that we will here be concerned with here is a Causative/Resultative (C/R) construction illustrated below:

(39) a. Yang yul ba ra   yab-ri   wîna pi-n
          I   dog the ACC give-OBV:ACT.1 meat eat-PAST.3
          'I made the dog eat meat.' (MCD:29)
      b. Yang yul ba ra   yab-ri   wîna pi-ras
          I   dog the ACC give-OBV:ACT.1 meat eat-NEG
          'I didn't make the dog eat meat.' (MCD:29)

Although this looks superficially like a chaining construction, the treatment of the second, negative example provides evidence that it is quite different. Here the negative appears on the final verb (with consequent neutralization of person, tense and aspect distinctions), which one would think of as subordinate from a semantic point of view. But nonetheless the semantic scope of the negation is the entire assertion. With chaining construction, on the other hand, the scope of the negative is restricted to its own verb (both final and nonfinal verbs can be negated (Salamanca 1988:314)). (b) above has no sensible chaining interpretation, but there are other instances of the construction where both C/R and chaining interpretations are available:

(40) Witin ai pruk-an   kauhw-ras
       He   me hit-OBV:ACT.3 fall-NEG
       'He hit me and I didn't fall down.'/
       'He didn't knock me down.' (MVSQ:26)

Various further peculiarities of the Causative/Resultative construction will be discussed below.

There is a considerable further variety of serialization constructions, including aspectual, associated motion, benefactive and further types, surveyed in (Salamanca 1988:331–341). Here are a few examples:[19]

(41) a. in-i   yab-an
          weep-PROX give-PAST.3
          '(S)he wept for her/him.' (ELM:336)

---

[19]The final verb in (b) has the effect of pluralizing some argument, preferentially the subject.

    b. pul-i   dim-i   bal   aik-i   bangwh-an
       play-PROX enter-PP come-PROX give.me-PROX be full-PAST.3
       'They pretended to come in 'on me'.' (ELM:337)

Here we will analyse only the causatives. It should not be assumed that our analysis will apply without modification to the other types, since these are likely to involve quite different configurations.

As indicated by the examples (39) and (40), the semantic range of the Causative/Resultative construction spans both causative and resultative uses, and it can also express a permissive:

(42) Witin yang ra   ai swi-n   skul   ra wa-ri
      He   me   ACC me let-OBV:ACT.3 school to go-PAST.1
      'He let me go to school.' (MCC:203)

Because of the permissive reading in particular, we shall assume that the C/R construction has an LCS in which the second, Effect clause functions as an argument of the first, Cause clause.

Causative verbs such as **yabaia** 'give' and **swiaia** 'let' (cited in the infinitive form) will therefore have LCSs that are similar to those we have already proposed for the Romance languages. But a wide and not yet delineated range of verbs can also occur as the Cause verb, as illustrated in (40). We propose that these structures are produced with the aid of a lexical rule that has the effect of adding a Caused State argument to a verb, although we won't make any specific proposals as to how it works (but see (Bittner 1997)).

On this proposal for LCS, the Cause (first) clause will be the semantic head, while the Effect (second) clause is semantically a complement. But from the point of view of various other lines of grammatical evidence, the reverse seems to be true: the Effect clause acts as the head, hosting for example negation, while the Cause clause acts like some kind of subordinate element, such as an adjunct. In the following subsections we will examine various aspects of this 'head-switching' behavior.

2.2 Equivocal Headship

The most striking feature of the C/R construction is its equivocality in terms of headship; from a semantic point of view the Cause clause looks like the head, while in terms of the morphosyntactic features of the verbs, it is the Effect clause that looks like the head. Here we will focus on these issues of headship.

We have already noted that negation on the Effect clause can have semantic scope over the whole proposition. This effect extends to licensing polarity items in the Cause clause:

(43) a. upla   kumi sin   ai swi-n   dim-ras
       person one   'also' me let-OBV:ACT.3 enter-NEG
       'No-one let me enter.' (MVSC:11)

     b. upla   kumi sin   yul ra   mun-ka   mai sam-bia
       person one   'also' dog ACC 'give'-OBV:VRT.3 you bite-FUT.3
       apia
       NEG
       'No-one will get the dog to bite you.' (CC:58)

Here **upla kumi sin** is a negative polarity item meaning 'no-one'. Although it appears in the Cause clause, it is licensed by the negation in the Effect clause. By contrast, licensing of a polarity item in a nonfinal clause by a negative in the final clause does not seem to be possible when the nonfinal verb doesn't support a Causative/Resultative interpretation:

(44) a.   yang sula kum kaik-ri   plap-ras
       I   deer a   see-OBV:ACT.1 run-NEG
       'I saw a deer and it didn't run.' (MVSC:11)

     b. *upla   kumi sin   sula kum kaik-an   plap-ras
       person one   'also' deer one   see-OBV:ACT.3 run-NEG
       'No-one saw a deer that didn't run.' (MVSC:12)

A further manifestation of the syntactic headship of the Effect verb can be seen when a C/R construction is embedded as an infinitival complement. In this case, the infinitival inflection appears on the Effect rather than the Cause verb:

(45) Yang want sna   mai-k(ri)-ka   kauhw-aia
     I   want be.PRES.1 you-make-OBV:ACT.1 fall-INF
     'I want to make you fall.' (MCD:3)

The infinitive form is strongly (but not, apparently, exclusively (Hale 1989:194)) associated with clauses with controlled ('proximate') subjects. Here however the control associated with the use of the infinitive is not of the subject of the verb actually bearing the marker, but of the Cause (nonfinal) verb. This corroborates both the semantic headship of the Cause verb and the headship of the Effect verb for at least some syntactic purposes.

Within a transformational framework, these data seen so far might be analysed in terms of a proposal by (Salamanca 1988:327-328), whereby the Cause clause is indeed the syntactic head, and the Effect clause its complement, but the apparent reversal in status is produced by a rule raising the Effect verb into the Cause clause's INFL position, which is clause-final:

(46) $[\ldots \mathrm{V}\ [\ldots t_i]\ \mathrm{V}_i\text{-INFL}]$

Some further process would also be required to place a reduced copy of the main clauses INFL features onto the main verb (this might be seen as a variant of Tense-Lowering in English, differing in that what is placed onto the V is a reduced version of the original in INFL, and the original is not deleted).

Such an analysis might also be technically feasible in LFG-like theories, but would involve rather awkward stipulations, which one would expect to be diachronically fragile, in order to prevent the main verbs from showing full main clause-inflection. There is however some further evidence that this is the wrong approach, in the form of some very intriguing data concerning question-answer pairs. If the Effect clause of a question contains a *Wh*-word, the answer can consist of the Effect clause repeated with an appropriate answer substituted for the *Wh*-word. In the presently available data, most of the clearest examples are Sumu rather than Miskitu, so below we provide one example from Miskitu and one from Sumu:

(47) Q: Papikam mai-k-an   wîna ba dia   ni   klak-ram
      father.2 you-Cause-OBV:ACT meat the what with cut-PAST.2
      (ki)
      Q
      'What did your father have you cut the meat with?'
   A: Skiru ni   klak-ri
      knife with cut-PAST.1
      'I cut with a knife.' (MCD:8, Miskitu)

(48) Q: Mâmahma mâtak   ai   rumpidam
      mother.2   you.cause.OBV.3 what throw.PAST.2
      'What did your mother make you throw?'
   A: Kuhbil rumpikda
      knife   throw.PAST.1
      'I threw a knife.' (MCD:8, Sumu)

The echoing of part of the Effect clause is hard to reconcile with an analysis in which the Effect verb raises into the Cause=Main clause as suggested in (46). It is also difficult to reconcile with the idea that the Effect clause is itself subordinate rather than main.

On the other hand, if the Effect clause is the main clause and the Cause clause subordinate, then the phenomenon is quite reminiscent of the treatment of adjuncts in English, which can be omitted from an answer when present in the question:

(49) Q: When you were in Philadelphia, what did you do?
   A: I went to the Art Museum.

Thus ellipsis (which is optional) seems to give results consistent with the treatment of the morphosyntactic features, indicating that the Effect clause is the syntactic head.

But there are other phenomena that suggest grammatical headship for the Cause clause. In (45) above, for example, the Cause subject of the complement of **want sna** is crucially coreferential with the subject of *want sna* itself; such coreference is usual when the complement appears in the infinitive (Hale 1989:194, Salamanca 1988:281). Likewise in the imperative, it is the subject of the Cause clause that is 2nd person, not the Effect clause. In Miskitu, but not in Sumu, there is a further indication of the headship of the Cause clause, which is that the imperative morphology is expressed on the Cause clause, not the head, running counter to the pattern we have seen elsewhere:[20]

(50) a. Mun-s   bal-aia/bal-bia
         cause-IMP.2 come-INF/come-FUT.3
         'Make him come!' (MCD:6)
      b. Swi-s   bal-bia
         let-IMP.2 come-FUT.3
         'Let him come.' (MCD:6)

In Sumu on the other hand the imperative morphology appears on the Effect verb, with the Cause verb in the appropriate Obviative form:

(51) a. Kumhpam   wârang/wangh
         cause.OBV.2 come.INF/come.FUT.3
         'Make him come!' (MCD:6)
      b. Dâpam   wangh
         let.OBV.2 come.IMP.3
         'Let him come.'

What is therefore needed is an analysis that will allow us to reconcile these contradictory indications about grammatical headship. We show below how our concept of differential spreading of different kinds of attributes provides this.

2.3 Differential Spreading

In the analysis, we will assume that the Causative/Resultative constructions consist of an S sitting over two S's. It is clear that this structure could be elaborated with further functional projections such as IP, but we will not pursue such elaborations here:

---

[20] Hale's 'Miskitu Causative Constructions' problem set (MIT, 1989, problem #3 24.915) gives future as the form of the second verb, while MCD seems to have some vacillation between the future and the infinitive. The problem set also notes that some Miskitu speakers tend to put infinitive marking on the Cause rather than the Effect verb as well.

(52)

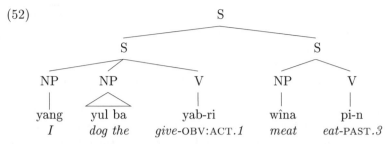

To account for how the morphosyntactic features work we need to have the second clause sharing μ with the whole construction (so that for example if a syntactic principle mandates infinitive mood, this will be spelled out on the Effect verb). On the other hand the Effect clause needs to function as a kind of semantic complement of the the Cause clause, without making this the head for all purposes. We can achieve this by having the Cause-clause share α with its mother, while the Effect clause is introduced as an ARG (and therefore on the α-projection). The resulting partially annotated version of (52) will be:

(53)

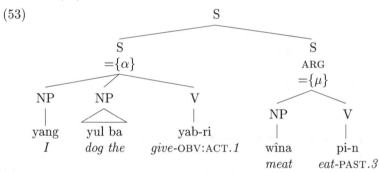

What about ρ? The indications are somewhat equivocal. It is clear that ρ cannot be shared across the whole construction, since the Cause and Effect clauses need to have different subjects. One might suggest that the properties of control infinitives and imperatives indicate that ρ should be shared between the top S and the Effect clause, but on the other hand cross-linguistically these phenomena are frequently defined over some kind of argument-structure, corresponding to our α rather than over the grammatical relations constituting ρ (Manning 1996a). Since we already have α shared between the top S and the Cause clause, further sharing of ρ here is not obviously necessary. There is furthermore the fact noted above that the Cause clause can be omitted in answers to questions (example (47) above), which suggests that the Cause clause should be seen as some kind of adjunct in terms of grammatical relations, with the effect clause being the ρ-head, and therefore sharing ρ with the top S. It seems to us that more descriptive work on the language will be needed to progress with this issue.

What then of the problem of imperatives illustrated in (50), where the imperative morphology is spelled out on the Cause rather than the Effect verb? One consideration is that there will already be need for sharing of the feature distinguishing Virtual from Actual forms (Future vs. Nonfuture) between the top S and the Cause clause. One might consider extending this limited sharing to include the features distinguishing the imperative, but this would not manage to suppress imperative marking on the Effect verb (this is a case where the idea of Movement seems to fit well).

What we suggest instead is that in Miskitu the imperative feature is 'mislocated' on the α-projection. This will cause it to be expressed on the Cause clause but not the Effect clause. This will be a marked deviation from the usual assignment of features to projections, found in Miskitu but not in Sumu.

We conjecture that the explanation for this mislocation lies in the course of acquisition; since the structure of the Miskitu C/R construction is somewhat unusual, children might go through a phase in which they analyse them as subordination constructions with the Effect clause serving as complement, providing a route for imperatives marked in accord with this kind of structure to find their way into learners' data. Such forms can then be accommodated into the mature grammar by putting the imperative features into a different projection than they would normally appear on.

2.4 The Argument-Structure

Although we have described how the α-structures of Causative verbs in Miskitu are to spread, we have not been explicit about what they are. The ones we will propose are very similar to those of Romance and Tariana, with one very important difference: there will be no fusion of the TERMS lists. Rather the Cause and Effect verbs each have their own independent TERMS-lists and grammatical relations. This has not been brought out in the examples so far, because the Causee has always been expressed in the Cause clause, but it is also possible to express it in the Effect clause, or even to express it as a full NP in the Cause clause and a pronoun in the Effect clause (but the reverse does not seem to be possible):

(54) a. Yang tuktan ba ra   mun-ri   plun atk-an
        I   child the ACC cause-OBV:ACT.1 food buy-PAST.3

     b. Yang tuktan ba ra   mun-ri   witin plun atk-an
        I   child the ACC cause-OBV:ACT.1 he   food buy-PAST.3

     c. Yang mun-ri   tuktika   ba plun atk-an
        I   cause-OBV:ACT.1 child.CONSTR the food buy-PAST.3
        'I had the child buy food.'

In fact, as noted by Bittner (1997) there is not even a clear requirement that the object of the Cause clause be coreferential with the Agent of the effect Clause. In (a) below the Cause object is coreferential with the Effect object, while in (b), the possessor of the Cause object is coreferential with the Effect subject:

(55) a. upla   kumi sin   mai   mun-an   yul mai
      person one 'also' you(OBJ) cause-OBV:ACT.3 dog you(OBJ)
      sam-ras kan
      bite-NEG PAST.3
      'Nobody will get you to be bitten by the dog.' (CC:58)

   b. Witin yul-i   ra   pruk-ka   yang law-aia   want sna
      he   dog-my ACC hit-OBV:ACT.3 I   angry-INF want PRES.3
      'He wants to make me angry by hitting my dog.'

In these examples, the negative polarity subject in (a) and the infinitival marking in (b) indicate that these are 'serializing' rather than mere clause-chaining constructions, but the common pattern of Cause object= Effect subject does not hold.

A further kind of example where the shared argument is neither a subject nor an Agent in the Effect clause arises with expressions for certain physiological states, where a nominal relevant to the state is the syntactic subject, and the Experiencer of the state the object:

(56) a. Li   di-n   wan dauki-sa
      water drink-NOM us   affect-PRES.3
      'We are thirsty.'
      (lit.: drinking water affects us)

   b. Naha warkka na wan mun-ka   li   di-n   wan
      this work this us do-OBV:VRT.3 water drink-NOM us
      dauk-bia
      affect-FUT.3
      'This work will make us thirsty.' (MCC:6)

In fact, there is even a Sumu example with no shared argument at all:

(57) Kârak   ârasyang   dai,   yang alas âranayang
     he.laugh.OBV.3 laugh.NEG.1 PAST.3, I   self laugh.PAST.1
     'He didn't laugh me into laughing, I laughed on my own.' (MCD:37, Sumu)

Here the continuation indicates that in spite of the position of the negative marker, what is being negated is not the fact of my laughing, but that his laughing is the cause of it.

All of this shows that there is no solid requirement for one of the Cause verb's arguments to be identified with one of those of the effect verb—not a surprise given that the TERMS-lists are not being merged in any way. What there do seem to be are some tendencies for coreference between Cause and Effect arguments, which are perhaps based on semantic requirements for the existence of causal relationships.

So we can now propose for basic causative verbs an α-structure like this:

$$(58) \begin{bmatrix} \text{LCS} & \text{Cause}(X,Y,Z) \\ \text{TERMS} & \langle X,Y \rangle \\ \text{ARG} & \begin{bmatrix} \text{LCS} & Z \end{bmatrix} \end{bmatrix}$$

Since the causer S shares its α-projection with the mother, this material becomes part of the α-projection of the mother. But then, since the feature-structure of the Effect clause is introduced by the annotated tree (for example, (53)) as the value of mother's ARG, the LCS of the Effect clause will be unified with the Cause-verbs ARG-value, and will thus wind up providing the semantic value for the Z slot in the LCS of the Cause clause.

Suppose for example that the Effect clause of (53) gets the following α-projection:

$$(59) \begin{bmatrix} \text{LCS} & \text{Eat}(X, Y) \\ \text{TERMS} & \langle X,Y \rangle \end{bmatrix}$$

The α-projection for the top mother S will then be:

$$(60) \begin{bmatrix} \text{LCS} & \text{Cause}(X,Y,\text{Eat}(V, W)_Z) \\ \text{TERMS} & \langle X,Y \rangle \\ \text{ARG} & \begin{bmatrix} \text{LCS} & Z \\ \text{TERMS} & \langle V,W \rangle \end{bmatrix} \end{bmatrix}$$

Surprisingly, despite the integration of the Cause and Effect α-projections, their TERMS-lists remain distinct, and the syntax does not enforce any particular pattern of coreference requirements on the arguments (although additional constraints could be imposed, if there were reason to do so). Furthermore, each TERMS-list meets linking theory on its own, and therefore the grammatical relations assigned in the Cause and Effect clauses remain distinct.

2.5 A 'Movement' Effect

Amongst the many loose ends in this treatment, one phenomenon of particular interest is that participants in the Effect clause seem able to appear in the Cause-clause. This is especially characteristic of question-words, and sometimes but not necessarily answers to such questions:

(61) Q: Yaptik-am dia   mai   mun-an   atk-ram
      mother-2   what you(OBJ) cause-OBV:ACT.3 buy-PAST.3
      'What did your mother make you buy?'

    A: Mamik-i ai-mun-an   radiu kum atk-ri
      mother-1 me-cause-OBV:ACT.3 radio a   buy-PAST.3
      'My mother had me buy a radio.' (MCD:23)

Here is a series of formulations of the question 'What did your father make you cut the meat with' in order of decreasing naturalness[21]

(62) a. Papik-âm dia   ni   mai-k-n   wîna ba
      father-2   what with you-Cause-OBV:ACT.3 meat ACC
      klak-ram   ki?
      cut-PAST.2 Q
      'What did your father make you cut the meat with?'

    b. Papikam wîna ba dia ni maikan klakram ki?

    c. Papikam maikan dia ni wîna ba klakram ki?

  Possible answers include:

(63) a. ai-k-n   kisura ni   klak-ri
      me-Cause-OBV:ACT.3 knife   with cut-PAST.1
      'I cut it with a knife.'[22]

    b. kisura ni aikan klakri

    c. kisura ni

The form of the (a) answer confirms that in the (a) form of the question, the *Wh*-phrase is being construed as the instrument of the Effect rather than of the Cause verb; the position of the Effect patient is likewise variable.

If the Effect clause were taken as some kind of complement, these phenomena might be treated as instances of some kind of 'Raising' process whereby constituents of a complement clause can be lifted into the matrix, but we have already rejected such an analysis. But our approach does in fact support an analysis that is very similar in spirit, because the Effect-clause is similar to a complement in that it is introduced as the value of ARG in the sentence structure. We can exploit this fact by introducing these 'Raised' NPs with composite grammatical functions, such as ARG OBJ or ARG OBL, similar to what has sometimes been proposed for components of XCOMPs that are not appearing in the appropriate VP. This analysis predicts that the conceptual components of the Cause and Effect clauses will have a considerable capacity to intermingle freely in the c-structure of the Cause clause, while maintaining the case-marking and agreement behavior

---

[21] Checked by Danilo Salamanca with two consultants; the last two are described as 'hard to get', various irrelevant meanings due to ambiguity ignored.

[22] This is the preferred answer to the first (and best) formulation of the question.

appropriate to the clause that they serve as TERMS-members in. It remains to be seen if this prediction will stand up to aggressive testing.

Another area which needs to be looked into more carefully is the grammar of the consecutive constructions. For example, do they have sharing of μ between the final clause (which carries full tense-marking) and the top S? And if they do, why doesn't a negated final verb take scope over the whole construction? We hope that by providing a straightforward treatment of the basic properties of the most theoretically problematic of these constructions, we will have made it easier to progress to an understanding of the whole system.

3 A perspective on serial verbs

In the previous two sections we have analysed two kinds of so-called 'Serial Verb Constructions'. Although they have both been given this label by the people working on them, and in the case of Misumalpan, the characterization has been accepted by others (Durie 1997:333), they are very different from each other, and also very different from the most-studied kinds of constructions to which the label has been applied, which are constructions that we will label 'VP-serializations', widespread in West African, Carribean Creole, Oceanic, and South-East Asian languages.[23] After a brief comparison of VP-serializations with the constructions we have been analysing, we will make some general observations about the general notion of SVC, and what we think that our architecture has to contribute to the investigation of these constructions.

3.1 'VP-serializations'

VP-serializations are illustrated here by some examples from Sranan, an English-based creole spoken in Surinam (Sebba 1987):

(64) a. A waka go na wowoyo
He walk go LOC market
'He walks to the market.'

b. Kofi naki Amba kiri
Kofi hit Amba kill
'Kofi struck Amba dead.'

c. Mi sa opo yu poti na abra liba
I FUT lift you put LOC over the river
'I shall lift you over the river.'

d. Dagu piri en tifi gi en
dog peel his teeth give him
'Dog bared his teeth at him.'

---

[23] See Sebba (1987), Crowley (1987), Baker (1989), Wilawan (1993), Bodomo (1997) and several of the papers in Lefebvre (1991) for representative discussions of this type.

e. No teki baskita tyari watra
   NEG take basket carry water
   'Don't carry water with a basket.'

There seems to be a widespread consensus that these constructions involve combinations of some kind of VP-like constituent. The verbs arguably head distinct phrasal projections, with the second verb heading a constituent that can contain a complement, but not an overt subject, and also lacking independent aspect, tense or mood.[24]

This construction differs from the Tariana SVCs where the verbs appear to be grouped under a single V constituent. Tariana SVCs fall into the general category of 'nuclear serialization' on Foley and Olson's (1985) theory, where verbs are serialized but the rest of the clausal environment is shared, while VP-serialization constitutes a looser type which they call 'core serialization', meaning that the verbs have independent core arguments, but share peripheral arguments and operators. The Misumalpan constructions on the other hand appear to be of a looser type than has been previously recognized, wherein each verb heads a c-structural clause that is also able to have its own overt subject.[25] VP-serializations thus seem to be intermediate in tightness between the two types we have analysed.

It would be desirable to have an analysis of (the very likely various kinds of) VP-serialization within our framework, but there are a number of issues that would need to be attended to in order to produce a well-motivated one. First we would need to establish the character of the grammatical relations in these constructions. The fact that each V can appear with an object suggests that perhaps each is in its own domain of ρ-sharing. So in the 'instrumental' serialization of (64e), the first verb, glossed 'take', will take the instrument as its OBJ, while the second, glossed 'carry' will take the theme as its OBJ.

On the other hand a prominent feature of these constructions is the 'object-sharing' effect, whereby an argument is clearly shared between both verbs, but expressed in only one of the putative VPs. This is illustrated in (64b,c), where the second verbs would appear in an independent clause with their own objects, and are clearly ascribing a semantic role to the referent of the object of the first V. Nonetheless, in Sranan, the second verb cannot take an overt object without altering the interpretation of the construction

---

[24]However, an object is often shared between the two verbs, as discussed at especial length by Baker (1989) and Collins (1997), though see Durie (1997) for some criticism.

[25]The appearance of independent subjects would seem to fall within the definition of core juncture within Foley and Olson's (1985) Role and Reference Grammar account, though in practice the term has been used to refer to VP-serialization. An inability to clearly distinguish these two types seems to be a weakness of the RRG theory of juncture.

(Sebba 1987).[26] This would be explained immediately if the grammatical relations were shared between the two verbs, in the manner of Tariana, in spite of each verb appearing under its own phrasal projection of V. But to make this work, we would have to come up with some way to associate each NP with the correct V in the linear order. And although full sharing of the GRs is *prima facie* plausible for Sranan, it is clearly not for some other VP-serializations, such as those of Paamese (Crowley 1987). Here both verbs in an VP serialization show independent inflection for subject and object GR's (and transitivity marking in the case of transitive verbs meeting certain phonological conditions), so an analysis in terms of full sharing of ρ is impossible.

A perhaps more fundamental problem arises with the modes of semantic composition in these constructions. In our treatments of Tariana and Miskitu, we have restricted ourselves to constructions that can be seen as semantically equivalent to complementation (or nonboolean coordination, in the case of Tariana symmetric SVCs). But there are many semantic types of SVC construction for which this seems quite inappropriate, one of the more spectacular cases being '*take*-serializations' used to express the Theme of transfer verbs such as 'give', illustrated here for Haitian Creole (Déchaine 1988):

(65) Emil pran liv   la   bay Mari
      Emil take book Det give Mary
      'Emil gave the book to Mary.'

Semantic analyses of these kinds of constructions have tended to assume some kind of merger of semantic structures, whereby one verb expresses the Theme and the other a Recipient/Goal (see especially Lefebvre (1989) and Bodomo (1997)), of a kind that seems fundamentally different from what is found with complementation or subordination.

Since our framework has different classes of attributes that are shared in different ways, we could propose an analysis whereby in terms of grammatical relations and c-structural configuration, *take*-serializations looked like VP-complement structures (albeit of a reduced from, without independent tense or polarity), with anaphoric control of the subject, and each verb having its own object:

---

[26]This seems to be characteristic of the West African and Carribean constructions. In South-East Asian languages, anaphoric ellipsis of NPs is more aggressive and so the facts are less clear, with the result that a wider range of constructions, such as for example purposives, tend to acquire the SVC label (Wilawan 1993).

(66)

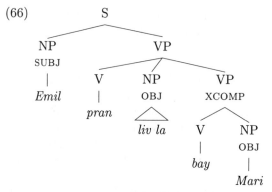

Nonetheless, in spite of this high degree of syntactic autonomy, the LCS-values could be combined quite tightly, each verb making overlapping claims about what the arguments are doing. The *take*-verb might for example say that its SUBJ causes the Theme to go somewhere, without saying where, while the *give* verb says that its subject causes something to go to its OBJ, without saying what:

(67)

pran: $\begin{bmatrix} \text{LCS} & \text{Cause}(X, Y, \text{Go}(Y, -)) \\ \text{TERMS} & \langle X, Y \rangle \end{bmatrix}$

bay: $\begin{bmatrix} \text{LCS} & \text{Cause}(X, -, \text{Go}(-, \text{To}(Y))) \\ \text{TERMS} & \langle X, Y \rangle \end{bmatrix}$

(The linking theory will associate first and second positions on the TERMS-list with SUBJ and OBJ grammatical functions, respectively.) The two LCS-values can be combined by having an equation such as ($\uparrow$ LCS) = ($\uparrow$ XCOMP LCS) in the lexical entry of the *take*-verb, so that the α-projection for the top S, VP and V of (66) would wind up being:

(68) $\begin{bmatrix} \text{LCS} & \overbrace{\text{Cause}(X, Y, \text{Go}(Y, \text{To}(Z)))} \\ \text{TERMS} & \langle X, Y \rangle \\ \text{XCOMP} & \begin{bmatrix} \text{LCS} & - \\ \text{TERMS} & \langle X, Z \rangle \end{bmatrix} \end{bmatrix}$

The alternative is to more follow the intuitions of Sebba (1987:98) and Durie (1997) that even these VP-serializations are still only one clause. The evidence for this is partly intuition, but it encompasses the observations that (i) the whole SVC describes a single event, (ii) verbs after the first do not have an overt subject of their own, (iii) there is shared tense, aspect, and mood marking throughout the SVC, (iv) later verbs (often) share objects as well as subjects with earlier verbs, and (v) overall the array of arguments in an SVC resembles that of a single clause in other languages (e.g., while (65) involves two verbs, the resultant argument array of agent, theme, and recipient is normal for a single clause). While (i) and (ii) can be adequately explained under the XCOMP analysis, (iii–v) are more suggestive of there being sharing of grammatical relations via $=\{\rho\}$, just as in the nuclear serializations of Tariana.

Under this analysis, the c-structure and α-projection would be roughly as in (69). The verb **bay** 'give' would here be analyzed as taking three term arguments (as in Baker (1989)). Two of these arguments would be shared with arguments of the first verb, and so the complete merger of the TERMS lists of the two verbs would yield a TERMS list for the clause which also has three members.

(69) a.

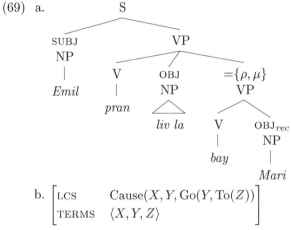

b. $\begin{bmatrix} \text{LCS} & \text{Cause}(X, Y, \text{Go}(Y, \text{To}(Z))) \\ \text{TERMS} & \langle X, Y, Z \rangle \end{bmatrix}$

Both these accounts have some initial plausibility. The crucial question is how to show whether VP-serialization really does or does not have full grammatical relations sharing. If full sharing cannot be motivated – and at present there is no solid evidence for compression of two grammatical relation arrays into one, such as arguments appearing in the wrong place as in Romance, then the goal would be to explain more comprehensively the ways in which the LCSs of the verbs nevertheless combine, and how grammaticalization is possible under such an account. If these SVCs can be shown to share a single array of grammatical relations, then we would need to introduce a method of nevertheless managing to constrain the placement of objects, so that in (65), the theme must appear after **pran** 'take' and the recipient after **bay** 'give'. One possibility for this is to revive the notion of *semantic dependence* which Andrews and Manning (1993) used to constrain clitic placement possibilities in Romance. It still seems plausible to us that semantic dependence is needed within a general theory of complex predicates. For example, note that on Butt's account of Urdu permissives, there is really no explanation of why the OBJ and the OBJ$_{go}$ cannot be swapped in example (2.10b), but they cannot. Semantic dependence could be used to give an account of this. So, in short, the proper analysis of VP-serializations remains a topic for further research.

3.2 The Notion 'SVC'

In the face of the diverse data of this chapter, can we find any unified concept of 'SVC'? Although many attempts have been made to define this notion, they all seem to wind up leaving out constructions for which the label has been accepted, or including ones such as complex predicates for which it is generally rejected. For example Butt (1995:225) suggests that the difference between 'serial verbs' and 'complex predicates' is that complex predicates refer to a single event while serial verbs stack multiple events into a single, complex event. But we have seen both Tariana and Miskitu SVCs having the same functions as Romance and Urdu complex predicates. Other workers such as Baker (1989) and Collins (1997) have deliberately chosen rather narrow characterizations of the term, proposing that their narrow characterization refers to a significant type of construction while the wider usages may perhaps not, but this still leaves open the question of what predisposes researchers to use the SVC label in the wider sense in which it tends to be employed. Our belief is that there is indeed no distinctive synchronic grammatical mechanism (such as a 'serialization parameter') that characterizes these constructions. Rather there are a number of circumstances which tend to lead to the label being applied. Some of these are rather superficial in terms of the nature of the underlying generative mechanisms involved in the constructions, but are nonetheless, we suggest, quite significant for the diachronic development of the languages. SVCs thus wind up being a genuine linguistic category, although not one that is appropriately defined solely in terms of generative grammatical mechanisms.

The first of these circumstances is that there actually be some complex of overt morphosyntactic properties (morphology and word-order) that constitute an identifiable multi-verb construction from a descriptivist's point of view. For example a sequence of homogeneously-person-marked verb forms in a sequence, uninterruptable by major constituents (Tariana), a sequence of non-embedded verb-forms with proximate/obviate marking, followed by a independent main verb, each perhaps with its own arguments (Miskitu), or a sequence of verbs perhaps with their own objects, but no individual overt subjects for the post-initial verbs (Haitian).

The second circumstance is that the verbs in the construction be required to share all or almost all of their 'peripheral' attributes (in the sense of (Foley and Van Valin 1984, Foley and Olson 1985) such as tense, mood, aspect and polarity (independent polarity seems to occur occasionally, but not tense or mood). This amounts to the requirement that the verbs be more tightly integrated than in a simple paratactic construction, and is perhaps what lies behind the common observation that the verbs in an SVC construction present a 'single event'.

These two circumstances fail to distinguish SVCs from complex predicates, or even from the bare infinitival complements of *make* and perception-verbs in English; this is accomplished by the next two criteria, the first of which is that the semantic uses of the construction extend beyond either complementation or coordination. In Haitian, for example, one of the standardly recognized SVC types is the Causative (Déchaine 1988:49):

(70) Emil bay Mari achte rad   la
     Emil give Mary buy   dress DET
     'Emil had Mary buy the dress.'

In appearance, this is indistinguishable from its English free translation, which is uncontroversially analysed as a complement construction (functional control by object, ECM, subject-to-object raising, etc., depending on the framework).

If Haitian had no similar-looking constructions for which a complementation semantics were clearly inappropriate, such as the *take*-serialization, it seems unlikely that (70) would be analysed any differently than its English translation. It is the use of the overt structural form to express semantics different from those of complementation that triggers the characterization of this construction as a type of serial verb. Similarly, if symmetric SVCs in Tariana were the only form of V–V construction in the language, it is unlikely that one would label them as a form of serial verb, rather than of coordination.

The fourth and final factor is that the morphosyntactic strategy used to mark the constructions should not look like either classical subordination (complementation with some kind of dependent-marking on the complement) or coordination (some technique also used to express boolean semantic combinations), but rather resemble a paratactic or consecutive clause structure. On these grounds, Romance complex predicates manage to escape the SVC label because they share the dependent-marking strategy of complementation (from which they are obviously diachronically derived, and with which they often alternate freely), and English non-boolean coordinate verbs (*John is kicking and screaming about the budget-cuts*) escape the SVC label because they have the superficial appearance of boolean coordination. Tariana symmetric SVCs get the label because they have no conjunction, and Haitian causatives get the label because they have no subordinator.

While these criteria do a pretty good job at picking out the constructions that tend to get the 'SVC' label, they do not seem to pick out any category that makes sense in terms of grammatical mechanisms. In particular, the details of marking have very little significance for the underlying grammatical analysis.[27] Since SVCs overlap in functionality with for example complex predicates, and at least some types seem to submit to analysis in terms of the same kind of theoretical mechanisms, one might propose that the SVC category is fundamentally a mistake: a disparate assortment of constructions that have been erroneously grouped under a single label by some (but certainly not all) linguists.

However we would suggest that perhaps there is something that unifies SVC constructions after all, but it is not the grammatical mechanisms employed in their analysis, but rather certain diachronic tendencies engendered by their form, in particular their lack of distinctive marking for coordination or subordination, and their resemblance to paratactic constructions. It is commonly suggested that SVC constructions tend to originate from paratactic constructions, for example VP-serializations from SOVOV sequences in SVO languages with liberal *pro*-drop, and nuclear (Tariana-like V-V) serializations from SOVV sequences in SOV languages (again with *pro*-drop) (Foley and Olson 1985:46-47). It is likewise very common for SVCs to be similar in superficial appearance, but different in less obvious grammatical properties, from some kind of paratactic or consecutive constructions (see Collins (1997) for recent discussion on Ewe; Salamanca (1988), Hale (1991) for discussion of Miskitu). The idea that SVC constructions tend to recruit from paratactic constructions would in fact explain one of the generalizations that Durie (1997) makes about SVCs, which is that they tend to be iconic, in that the order of verbs in the SVC reflects the order of sub-events in the complex event referred to by the SVC.

This view of SVCs allows us to treat the various kinds of SVCs, even ones that are rather similar in appearance, as being rather different in the underlying grammatical mechanisms they employ (and sometimes nondistinct from other kinds of constructions such as coordinate structures and complex predicates), while not losing an account of the tendencies which suggest that they should be recognized as a category. But the explanation of these tendencies is taken to have an essential diachronic dimension rather than being purely in terms of principles of synchronic grammatical structure.

---

[27] One could imagine variants of generative grammar in which they did, but in practice they do not, given the latitude that generative theories have to delete, insert and copy markers. Phenomena such as 'pseudo-coordination' in Mainland Scandinavian, where there are constructions that look like coordination but have the syntactic properties of complementation (Josefsson 1991, Wiklund 1996, Bodomo 1997), suggest strongly that this latitude is an empirically necessary property of generative theories, rather than a defect.

3.3 Conclusion

Our architecture is based on the idea of differential spreading of different classes of attributes, coupled with the separation between phrase structure and feature structures that is the hallmark of LFG. Because of this, it provides considerable freedom to express various combinations of morphosyntactic feature management, syntactic organization and semantic composition. The ability to express a wide range of semantic combinations with a single constituent structure configuration and vice versa is, we think, particularly significant for the study of serialization, since many discussions, such as Lefebvre (1989), Durie (1997), and Bodomo (1997) emphasize that the constructions seem to involve more types of semantic composition than those standardly associated with complementation and conjunction. We hope that our architecture will help linguists to produce straightforward accounts of what is actually found in languages, rather than trying to shoehorn the facts into one or another procrustean bed, and that the flexibility of the formal framework will also encourage the search for functional and historical explanations (which, by Occam's Razor, are inherently superior when available and well-motivated). Of course such flexibility is often seen as a vice in theoretical linguistics, the goal being a maximally restrictive linguistic theory, but this goal has to be balanced against the requirement of correctly describing what is actually present in languages. At present, a flexible framework for accurately specifying different forms of information spreading seems a good first achievement. Over time, it may prove possible to produce a typologically adequate substantive linguistic theory that further delimits what patterns of spreading actually occur.

5

Conclusions and Prospects

In this work we have had three interrelated aims. The first was to provide a better formal basis for the description of complex predicates and various other phenomena. There has been much recent work on complex predicates in LFG, but, to our minds, none of it has successfully spanned the gap between linguistic adequacy and formal soundness and rigor. While linguistic work has contained suggestions of formal mechanisms, they have, in general, been imprecise, full of problems, have involved special purpose mechanisms specific to one linguistic construction, or have often demonstrated several of these faults simultaneously, as we have attempted to document in Chapter 2. On the other hand, while formal work has been intrigued by the phenomena of complex predicates, and this has led to a number of proto-analyses, as documented in Appendix B, this interest has generally seen papers about the analysis of one example sentence. A more thorough consideration of the empirical domain of complex predicates reveals that these proposals do not at present deal adequately with major properties of complex predicates, such as respecting the tree structure, coping with complex predicates that add arguments and those that do not, and dealing with ancillary phenomena such as clitic placement and adverb scope. Often it seems problematic to extend the proposals to further data, and at any rate, the necessary work has not been done. This is not to say that all these papers do not all contain useful material. We have benefitted greatly from empirical work by the former group, and theoretical work by the latter group. In particular, in this monograph, we have picked up and deployed both the use of linear-logic glue-language semantics, and the notion of set restriction. But nevertheless, we have tried to fill the void between the two. We have put forward a formally sound and clean, general extension to LFG, which is usable in all places in linguistic theory where issues of multiple headship arise. Although we have mainly dwelt on complex predicates, such places are numerous, as is indicated by the interest in the notion of head in such recent work as that contained in Corbett et al. (1993), and we

113

briefly mentioned some other possible applications in the first chapter. We have then applied this proposal to analyzing complex verb constructions in a reasonably diverse range of languages in sufficient detail as to make restriction projections plausible as a device for treating all phenomena that come under the rubric of complex predicates.

At this point the first goal meets the second. While there has been a great deal of work on complex predicates in LFG, most of it has been typologically impoverished and has dealt with a limited range of cases from a limited range of languages. In particular, it has concentrated on causatives and causative-like constructions, and modal and similar light verbs. We feel that this leaves out an enormous range of the phenomena that a theory of complex predicates should deal with. In particular, the various coverb-verb constructions and serial verb constructions, which have been described in languages widespread across the globe, appear to be rather more varied and analytically challenging than the complex predicates found in the better studied Indo-European languages. Our goal here is to bring some of the syntactic rigor available within LFG (and generative grammatical theory more generally) to dealing with the substantive problems that are widespread in the descriptive literature. We have not been able to be comprehensive, but have tried to look in detail at two constructions that have gone under the serial verb construction label, and have briefly discussed a number of others. Our general conclusion is that there is no unity to the notion 'serial verb' at the level of syntactic analysis. The syntactic structure of Tariana serial verbs is miles apart from that of Miskitu serial verbs, and in particular, the syntax of Tariana SVCs seems rather closer to Romance complex predicates, which have not traditionally been thought of as serial verbs. We hope that a good role for our work, and for LFG in general, is in providing well-defined syntactic tools for analyzing the eye-witness reporting of descriptivists, without them feeling that they have to shoehorn their language into the straightjacket of some recent generative approaches. Here, we see particular promise in the flexible notions of head-ship and information spreading, and the consequent ability to dissociate various types of information, which our theory provides.

If there is any commonality to serial verbs, it is at a functional level, where all languages have similar pressures to express certain relationships between actors and the world, and functional concerns will lead there to be overlap in the means used and the restrictions on their use. Nevertheless, consonant with the leitmotif of LFG, we have argued that serial verb constructions often cover a number of different functional relationships that share the same phrase structure, while on the other side of the equation, the same functional relationship can be expressed by a number of different phrase structure configurations.

The one area where we have done enough concentrated work to be able to say something substantial is causatives, and developing the typology of causative relationships, in sync with adequate formal tools for their description, became our third aim. In the literature, it is generally accepted that there are four kinds of causative relationships. Semantic causation can be lexicalized in the meaning of a verb, as in the verb *show*, in either the English or Japanese examples in (1):

(1) a. I showed him the footprints in the sand.
   b. Taroo ga   Ziroo ni   e   o   mise-ta.
      Taro NOM Ziro DAT picture ACC show-PAST
      'Taroo showed a picture to Ziroo.'

Or causation can be expressed via a productive morphological derivation, such as in the Japanese and Chicheŵa causatives shown in (2).

(2) a. Yumiko ga   Ziroo ni   sono hon o   yom-ase-ta.
      Yumiko NOM Ziroo DAT that book ACC read-CAUS-PAST
      'Yumiko made/let Ziroo read that book.'
   b. mlīmi   a-ku-kémb-éts-a   mkángó ndakatūlo
      1.farmer 1S-PR-write-CAUS-FV 3.lion   9.poem
      'The farmer is making the lion write the poem.'

Thirdly, causation can be expressed in a multiclausal form using regular verb complementation, as in English:

(3) The farmer is making him plough the field.

The final type is monoclausal syntactic causatives, typified by Romance languages such as Italian here:

(4) Maria ha fatto riparare la   macchina a Giovanni
   Maria has made repair   the car   to Giovanni
   'Maria had Giovanni repair the car.'

As we discussed in Chapter 3, recent work has argued strongly that this last kind, although looking on the surface like other syntactic causatives, is in functional and argument structure much more akin to the morphological causatives of Japanese and Chicheŵa. This has tended to be problematic for incorporation-based accounts,[1] but different phrase structures generating basically the same feature structure is straightforward in our approach.

In Romance, an ARG-substructure is introduced in the syntax. In languages with overtly incorporational causatives, this kind of substructure is introduced in the morphology. The verb-stem of a causative is introduced as bearing an ARG function to the affix. Given this, we can propose for the Chicheŵa example in (2b), the word structure and feature structure

---

[1]For instance, Baker (1988:202–294) proposes a rather obscure and problematic notion of 'abstract incorporation (at LF)' (for the difficulties, see especially his fn. 37, p. 467).

shown in (5), and the analysis of Chicheŵa causatives is then parallel in all respects except surface form to that given in Chapter 3 for Romance.

(5) a.

$$
\begin{array}{c}
\text{V} \\
\overbrace{\qquad\qquad} \\
\begin{array}{cc}
=\{\rho\} & \textit{-ets} \\
(\uparrow \text{ARG}) = \downarrow \\
\text{V} \\
| \\
\textit{sak}
\end{array}
\end{array}
$$

b.
$$
\begin{bmatrix}
\text{SUBJ} & \begin{bmatrix}\text{LCS} & \text{Farmer}\end{bmatrix}^U \\
\text{OBJ} & \begin{bmatrix}\text{LCS} & \text{Lion}\end{bmatrix}^V \\
\text{OBJ} & \begin{bmatrix}\text{LCS} & \text{Poem}\end{bmatrix}^W \\
\text{LCS} & \text{Cause(U, V, Z)} \\
\text{TERMS} & \langle\text{U, V, W}\rangle \\
\text{ARG} & \begin{bmatrix}\text{LCS} & \text{Write(V, W)} \\ \text{TERMS} & \langle\text{V, W}\rangle\end{bmatrix}^Z
\end{bmatrix}
$$

In a sentence like (2b), the feature structures corresponding to the grammatical relations will be shared between the upper and lower levels of the feature structure of the verb, so that the overall feature structure will be the same as in a Romance causative, in spite of the major difference in morphological technique.

Our major addition to this typology has been to examine the realization of causatives via serial verb constructions.[2] We have argued that within the domain of serial verbs there are both monoclausal causatives and multiclausal causatives. The former have grammatical-relation and argument-structure configurations that again resemble those from Romance or languages with morphological causatives, while the latter are much more similar to English, except in the matter of surface form. Again we see how surface phrase structure differences can hide underlying similarity and vice-versa.

This outline of a typology shows both the ongoing strength of LFG, and the limitations of the original conception. The original idea was that although the surface phrase structure of languages varied greatly, universality of syntactic processes could be achieved at the level of f-structure. A study

---

[2] We have not dealt in detail here with small-scale differences in the grammatical behavior of causatives of the sort much discussed by Zubizarreta (1985), Baker (1988) and so on, but see Manning et al. (in press) and Manning and Sag (in press) for some relevant discussion in an HPSG context.

such as this shows that this is too much to hope for in many cases, since a phenomenon like causatives also allows multiple expressions at the level of grammatical relations, where a causative can be either monoclausal or bi-clausal. On the other hand, the clear separation of levels in LFG allows one to easily enunciate and make precise the levels of syntactic representation that *are* shared across languages, and the ones on which languages differ. We see in this ongoing advantage a formalism that not only holds great promise for empirical linguists, but for linguistic theory more generally.

In the future we hope to extend this work, both to use the concept of restriction projections in completely different areas of the grammar where notions of differential spreading arise, and in particular in further examination of the treatment of complex verb constructions, where much careful syntactic work remains to be done in teasing apart distinctions within the realm of what is descriptively known a serial verb constructions. For the present, we have shown how the LFG framework can be slightly re-engineered by making use of positive restrictions, a simple and general new formal device. This minor change maintains the traditional LFG goal of dividing information into different types, but puts it on a sounder formal footing, and allows better analyses of important empirical phenomena that have challenged the framework.

A

Glue Language Semantics

In this appendix we formulate a proposal for the semantic interpretation of our feature-structures based on the approach of 'glue-language semantics' put forth in Dalrymple et al. (1997),[1] henceforth DLPS. The principal motivation for this approach has been that it provides a smooth treatment of quantifier scope phenomena that are difficult to get right in other approaches, but for our purposes the main appeal is that it provides a straightforward way to account for the ambiguous interpretation of adjuncts in complex predicate constructions.

Glue-language semantics can be regarded as a way of generalizing the basic ideas of 'compositional semantics' so that they can work off the typically re-entrant and possibly even cyclic feature structures often found in current constraint- or unification-based theories. Compositional semantic approaches such as the original 'Montague Grammar' work nicely off of non-reentrant tree-structures: the semantic composition rules are defined so as to recursively climb a tree from the leaves to the root, deriving at each non-leaf stage a meaning for a mother from those of the daughters. The non-reentrancy (lack of shared substructures) in the tree implies that the meaning of each component of the sentence gets used once and once only, while non-cyclicity and rootedness implies that the derivation of a meaning will terminate with some sort of result for the root, which is naturally interpreted as a meaning for the whole. But if a feature-structure has reentrancies, it is not so clear how to get each semantic contribution to be used exactly once in the interpretation, and if there are cycles, it might be unclear exactly what the interpretation of the whole structure is supposed to be.

Glue-language semantics addresses these issues by using (the tensor fragment of) linear logic as the mechanism to control meaning-assembly. The basic idea of linear logic is that it accounts for resources: when a

---

[1] See Dalrymple et al. (1995a) and Dalrymple et al. (1993) for other sources on this general approach.

premise is used in a deduction, it is 'consumed', and therefore no longer available. This means for example that if our list of premises is (A, A) (two instances of A), we can't just conclude A. We could however conclude A if we had an additional premise $A \otimes A \multimap A$, $\otimes$ being 'linear conjunction', and $\multimap$ being 'linear implication'. This is because the rules for $\otimes$ allow two instances of A in the list of premises to be replaced by one instance of $A \otimes A$, and then the linear version of modus ponens will allow us to take this derived premise and the linear implication from the list of premises and to replace them with the consequent of the implication, A.

The property that a premise is normally consumed when used makes it easy to account for the fact that many linguistic elements seem to be interpreted in one of several different ways, but only one of those ways at a time. For example, the universally quantified object in 'somebody loves everybody' can have wide or narrow scope, but not two scopes at once. This effect is captured by having alternate conclusions derivable from the premises supplied by the grammatical structure of the sentence. But since the premises are consumed in the production of a conclusion, one or the other of the alternates can be derived, but not both at the same time.

DLPS assume a standard LFG projection architecture, comprising a c-structure, an f-structure that includes PRED-features, and a semantic projection that comes off of the f-structure. The basic ingredients for semantic interpretation are provided by the lexicon as 'meaning constructors', which are either atomic assertions saying something about the meaning of a linguistic object, or combinations of such assertions built with the linear logic connectives $\otimes$ and $\multimap$ and universal quantification. In the DLPS formulation, the semantic projection simply serves as a sort of staging area for the construction of semantic interpretations. Atomic meaning constructors are assertions using the binary connective '$\rightsquigarrow$' (glossed 'means') that relate objects on the semantic projection on the left to an expression in some semantic representation language on the right.[2] Some form of intensional logic has usually been the choice for the semantic representation language, although any format whereby complex structures can be built up by substitution into positions in simpler ones can be used. If the $\uparrow$ arrow designates the f-structure of the c-structure node a lexical item is interpreted under, '$\uparrow_\sigma$' will designate the semantic projection that gets associated with the mother node of a lexical item. Then the lexical entry for a proper noun such as *Mary* might be:

(1) *Mary* NP $(\uparrow \text{PRED}) = $ 'Mary'

$\quad\quad\quad\quad\quad\quad \uparrow_\sigma \rightsquigarrow Mary$

---

[2]In the theory of Dalrymple et al. (1997), '$\rightsquigarrow$' is subscripted with the type of the meaning expression, but this complication is unneeded and so omitted in this appendix.

This is supposed to induce in the linguistic structure a substructure that looks like this:

(2)
$$\phi \qquad\qquad\qquad \sigma$$
$$\text{NP} \dashrightarrow f:[\text{PRED} \quad \text{'Mary'}] \dashrightarrow f_\sigma:[\ ] \rightsquigarrow Mary$$
$$|$$
$$Mary$$

The objects in the semantic projection play a very minor role. These (frequently empty) attribute-value structures can be thought of as 'handles' for accessing the pieces of semantic structure. The pieces are then assembled by means of linear logic deductions, as described in greater detail below.

The meaning-constructor proposed above for *Mary* was atomic, while the meaning-constructors for verbs will typically be linear implications, with each argument represented by a conjunct in the antecedent. For a transitive verb such as *appoint*, the constructor might be:

(3)　*appoint*　V　$(\uparrow \text{PRED}) = \text{'Appoint'}$
$$\forall X, Y.(\uparrow \text{SUBJ})_\sigma \rightsquigarrow X \otimes (\uparrow \text{OBJ})_\sigma \rightsquigarrow Y \multimap$$
$$\uparrow_\sigma \rightsquigarrow appoint(X, Y)$$

The semantic constructor is a universal quantification on the variables X and Y, which range over the semantic specifications such as may be provided by the SUBJ and OBJ respectively, as indicated by the two premises $(\uparrow \text{SUBJ})_\sigma \rightsquigarrow X$ and $(\uparrow \text{OBJ})_\sigma \rightsquigarrow Y$, respectively. For a sentence such as *Mary appointed John*, one gets an f-structure as indicated below, where we use lowercase italic variables to represent the objects on the semantic projection, connected by dotted arrows to their corresponding f-structures. The meaning-constructors are written out below; note that the $\uparrow$-arrows have been replaced by the labels for the appropriate f-structures, as a result of lexical instantiation:

(4)
$$f:\begin{bmatrix} \text{SUBJ} & g:[\text{PRED} \quad \text{'Mary'}] \\ \text{PRED} & \text{'Appoint'} \\ \text{OBJ} & h:[\text{PRED} \quad \text{'John'}] \end{bmatrix} \begin{matrix} \dashrightarrow j \\ \dashrightarrow i \\ \dashrightarrow k \end{matrix}$$

$$\forall X, Y.(f\ \text{SUBJ})_\sigma \rightsquigarrow X \otimes (f\ \text{OBJ})_\sigma \rightsquigarrow Y \multimap f_\sigma \rightsquigarrow appoint(X, Y)$$
$$g_\sigma \rightsquigarrow Mary$$
$$h_\sigma \rightsquigarrow John$$

Now we can rewrite the meaning-constructors by replacing designators referring to objects on the semantic projection with the italic variables that have been chosen to tag them:

(5)　$\forall X, Y.j \rightsquigarrow X \otimes k \rightsquigarrow Y \multimap i \rightsquigarrow appoint(X, Y)$

$j \rightsquigarrow Mary$
$k \rightsquigarrow John$

By the linear logic rules for $\otimes$ and $\multimap$, these premises then allow us to conclude:

(6) $i \rightsquigarrow appoint(Mary, John)$

This deduction consumes all the premises, so that our original pool of assertions is replaced by (6) alone. And since this ascribes a meaning to the root S, it is taken to represent an interpretation (and in this instance the only interpretation) for the sentence.

We will comment briefly here on three features of this approach. The first is that the order of steps in the derivation does not matter. This example is too simple to be able to show this, but in general proofs can often do various subparts in different orders. What matters is the deducibility relationship itself, not the intervening steps in the derivation. Second, this mechanism expresses the intuition that all of the semantic material provided by the lexical entries must be used and therefore is able to produce the effects of the Coherence Constraint of standard LFG, while Completeness is captured by the requirement that a meaning actually get ascribed to the entire f-structure: Incomplete structures will be those lacking a premise needed to discharge an antecedent. Finally, it is important to point out that nothing depends on the details of the formal language chosen for expressing the meanings. All that matters is that they can be built up by substitution of expressions for variables.

In adapting DLPS's approach to our architecture, we will associate meaning constructors with the LCS attribute, rather than elements in a semantic projection. Previously the LCS-values have been the semantically relevant structures themselves; now they will be 'dummy objects', like the objects on the semantic projection in the DLPS architecture, which will appear on the left of a $\rightsquigarrow$ assertion, while the semantic material appears on the right.

A more significant difference will be that while in the DLPS approach, the meaning-constructors of predicates refer to grammatical relations such as SUBJ and OBJ (as illustrated above), ours will refer to positions on the TERMS-list (for term-arguments; for obliques we can continue to use oblique grammatical functions). This will allow the meaning-constructors for predicates to function either independently or in complex predicate constructions, without any need for lexical rules or similar devices. We continue to rely on a linking theory to connect the ρ-values to TERMS-lists positions.

For example, since a transitive verb such as *appoint* has a 2-place TERMS-list, its meaning-constructor will now be:

(7) $\forall X, Y.(\uparrow \text{TERMS HEAD LCS}) \rightsquigarrow X \otimes (\uparrow \text{TERMS REST HEAD LCS}) \rightsquigarrow Y$
$\qquad -\!\circ (\uparrow \text{LCS}) \rightsquigarrow appoint(X, Y)$

Notationally, this is rather cumbersome and off-putting, so to keep things from looking too much worse than they really have to, we will adopt a convention of implicit universal quantification so that outermost universal quantifiers can be dropped, and we will use the notation TERM.i to abbreviate TERMS REST^{i-1} LCS. We can now rephrase (7) as:

(8) $(\uparrow \text{TERM}.1) \rightsquigarrow X \otimes (\uparrow \text{TERM}.2) \rightsquigarrow Y -\!\circ (\uparrow \text{LCS}) \rightsquigarrow appoint(X, Y)$

Now consider a simple transitive clause, such as *Mary appointed John*. Here α and ρ will spread alike, so we can represent its structure rather informally as (9), where the feature-structure combines both α and ρ, and omits the others, and the meaning-constructors are written underneath. We also use the boxed number notation of PATR/HPSG to indicate which substructures in the full feature-structure occupy positions in the TERMS-list:

(9)

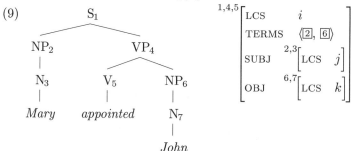

$(5 \text{ TERM}.1) \rightsquigarrow X \otimes (5 \text{ TERM}.2) \rightsquigarrow Y -\!\circ (5 \text{ LCS}) \rightsquigarrow appoint(X, Y)$
$(3 \text{ LCS}) \rightsquigarrow Mary$
$(7 \text{ LCS}) \rightsquigarrow John$

Now we can substitute the italic variables representing the LCS-values for their designators in the meaning-constructors above, whereby they may be rewritten as:

(10) $j \rightsquigarrow X \otimes k \rightsquigarrow Y -\!\circ i \rightsquigarrow appoint(X, Y)$
$\qquad j \rightsquigarrow Mary$
$\qquad k \rightsquigarrow John$

Again, the last two premises can be replaced by their linear conjunction, and then modus ponens allows us to replace the two premises with the single conclusion:

(11) $i \rightsquigarrow appoint(Mary, John)$

Since this gets assigned as the meaning for the c-structure root S_1, it represents an interpretation (in this case the only interpretation) for the whole structure.

This illustrates the interpretation of simple clauses (but without the quantificational phenomena that provide the original motivation for the approach). What of complex predicates? Consider the Catalan example:

(12) he   fet   beure el vi   a la Maria
     I.have made drink the wine to the Maria
     'I have made Maria drink the wine.'

Here the c-structure will be:

(13)

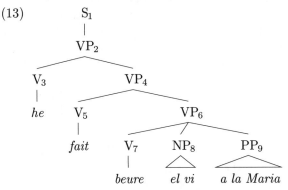

The c-structure is monoclausal, with the NP-argument material appearing as values of SUBJ, OBJ and OBJ_θ on the ρ-projection, shared between the correspondents of S and all of the verbal nodes. These ρ-projection values introduce LCS-values (in their α-projections) that we will tag with the variables l, m and n. This portion of the structure can be represented as:

$$(14) \quad {}^{1,2,3,4,5,6,7}\left[\begin{array}{l} \text{SUBJ} \quad {}^{10}\left[\text{LCS} \quad n\right] \\ \text{OBJ}_\theta \quad {}^{9,\cdots}\left[\text{LCS} \quad l\right] \\ \text{OBJ} \quad {}^{8,\cdots}\left[\text{LCS} \quad m\right] \end{array}\right]$$

The α-projection will on the other hand undergo considerably less compaction. Assuming an 'operator semantics' for the perfective auxiliary, the structure would be along the lines below, where for purposes of readability the intuitive significance of the material associated with each LCS-value is indicated in parentheses, and the TERMS-lists have been written out in full, redundantly, with the dotted lines indicating identities enforced by the lexical entries of the light verbs:

(15) [1,2,3]
$$\begin{bmatrix} \text{LCS} & i\ (Perf) \\ \text{TERMS} & \langle \boxed{10}, \boxed{8}, \boxed{9} \rangle \\ \\ \text{ARG} & {}^{4,5}\begin{bmatrix} \text{TERMS} & \langle \boxed{10}, \boxed{8}, \boxed{9} \rangle \\ \text{LCS} & j\ (Cause) \\ \text{ARG} & {}^{6,7}\begin{bmatrix} \text{TERMS} & \langle \boxed{8}, \boxed{9} \rangle \\ \text{LCS} & k\ (Drink) \end{bmatrix} \end{bmatrix} \end{bmatrix}$$

The meaning-constructor introduced by **beure** will be:

(16) $(7\ \text{TERM.1}) \leadsto X \otimes (7\ \text{TERM.2}) \leadsto Y \multimap (7\ \text{LCS}) \leadsto Drink(X, Y)$

Now suppose that the LCS's of the grammatical relations are associated with the meaning-constructors:

(17) a. $l \leadsto Maria$

  b. $m \leadsto wine$

  c. $n \leadsto me$

But since l is the LCS of the first item on structure 7's TERMS list, and m that of the second, (17) and (16) plus the fact that k is the LCS of structure 7 allow us to conclude:

(18) $k \leadsto Drink(Maria,\ Wine)$

This illustrates the interpretation of a pseudo-complement going through regardless of the grammatical relations and surrounding structure induced by the complex predicate.

Moving up to the causative, however, a complexity emerges. For this kind of causative we have been assuming a three-place predicate analysis, whereby the top argument of the pseudo-complement, the 'Causee', is taken to be the second argument of the causative predicate. This suggests a constructor such as:

(19) $(\uparrow \text{TERM.1}) \leadsto X \otimes (\uparrow \text{TERM.2}) \leadsto Y \otimes (\uparrow \text{ARG LCS}) \leadsto Z \multimap$
  $(\uparrow \text{LCS}) \leadsto cause(X, Y, Z)$

But this does not actually work, because TERM.2 (l as instantiated in our structure) also has to be supplied to the pseudo-complement to serve as its TERM.1. If it is consumed to serve as first argument of the Effect predicate, it will not be there to serve as the second argument of the Cause predicate, and vice-versa.

This requires a somewhat more complex meaning-constructor for the three-place Causative. We need to both plug in the Causee and manufacture a copy of the premise for use in the Effect pseudo-complement, which can be achieved with this constructor:[3]

(20) $(\uparrow \text{TERM.2}) \rightsquigarrow Y \multimap$
$$((\uparrow \text{TERM.1}) \rightsquigarrow X \otimes (\uparrow \text{ARG LCS}) \rightsquigarrow Z \multimap (\uparrow \text{LCS}) \rightsquigarrow cause(X, Y, Z))$$
$$\otimes (\uparrow \text{TERM.2}) \rightsquigarrow Y$$

In our structure, this will instantiate out to:

(21) $l \rightsquigarrow Y \multimap$
$$(n \rightsquigarrow X \otimes k \rightsquigarrow Z \multimap j \rightsquigarrow cause(X, Y, Z)) \otimes l \rightsquigarrow Y$$

Then (21) together with (17a) implies:

(22) $(n \rightsquigarrow X \otimes k \rightsquigarrow Z \multimap j \rightsquigarrow cause(X, Maria, Z)) \otimes l \rightsquigarrow Maria$

Now we can do a derivation by first using the Causee and Causative verb constructors to produce (22), and then using the resulting copy of the Causee constructor with the constructor of the Effect verb and its other argument(s) to produce (18). Then (17c) and (18) can be combined to give the left hand side of the linear implication in (22), which allows us to produce the consequent:

(23) $j \rightsquigarrow cause(me, Maria, drink(Maria, wine))$

This will then combine with the aspectual auxiliary's constructor, which we can assume to be:

(24) $(\uparrow \text{ARG LCS}) \rightsquigarrow Z \multimap (\uparrow \text{LCS}) \rightsquigarrow Perf(Z)$

to produce:

(25) $i \rightsquigarrow Perf(cause(me, Maria, drink(Maria, wine)))$

Note that because these deductions depend on the hierarchical structure of the α-projection, which is richer than that of ρ, the interpretation 'respects the tree' in Alsina's sense (unlike the analysis of Dalrymple et al. (1995a), which we discuss in Appendix B).

One advantage of taking a linear logic approach is that we can appropriate DLPS's main semantic results in the areas of quantification, intensionality and so on without significant effort, but a more immediately relevant result is that we can explain the interpretation of adjuncts in complex predicates, which frequently seem to be able to modify either the upper or the lower VP, as in the following example from Catalan:[4]

(26) He   fet   beure el vi   a contracor a la Maria
     I.have made drink the wine against heart to Maria
     'I have made Maria drink the wine against her/my will.'

---

[3]This use of duplication of a premise mirrors the treatment of pronouns in Dalrymple et al. (1997).
[4]Cited in Manning (1992), from Alex Alsina.

The ambiguous interpretation can be produced with the proposal for adjuncts in Dalrymple et al. (1993), in conjunction with the assumption that the ADJUNCTS-function belongs to the ρ-projection and is therefore shared between the upper and lower levels of the complex predicate structure.

Dalrymple et al. (1993) propose for the adverb *obviously* the following meaning-constructor (notation adapted to conform with DLPS):

(27) $\forall P.(\text{MODS} \uparrow)_\sigma \rightsquigarrow P \multimap (\text{MODS} \uparrow)_\sigma \rightsquigarrow Obviously(P)$

This makes use of 'inside out functional uncertainty' (Dalrymple 1993): the expression '(MODS $\uparrow$)' designates a feature-structure f such that $\uparrow$ is a member of f's MODS attribute. Adapting the notation of (27) to the present context, we get:

(28) $((\text{ADJUNCTS} \uparrow) \text{ LCS}) \rightsquigarrow P \multimap ((\text{ADJUNCTS} \uparrow) \text{ LCS}) \rightsquigarrow Obviously(P)$

What the constructor does is take some structure f that satisfies this condition, and applies the meaning of *obviously* to it. If there are multiple structures for which the feature-structure of an instance *obviously* is an ADJUNCTS member, the constructor can apply to any of them, but since it is consumed in the application, it applies to only one of them, resulting in an ambiguity. This will be the case for monoclausal complex predicates. In the full feature structure for (12), the grammatical relations SUBJ, OBJ, OBJ$_\theta$, and ADJUNCTS will appear at each level of the feature structure in (15), and the adjunct can modify at any level.

To account for **a contracor**, we need to deal with an additional complexity. Semantically, **a contracor** is a two-place predicate, in effect relating an individual to an action, and asserting that the individual performs the action, but against their will. The person who desires the action not to be performed is the TERM.1 of the verb to which the adverbial applies, whether this is the Causative verb or the Effect verb. Getting ahold of this value will require further reference to the feature structure of which the ADJUNCT is a member. Already in (28), there were two uses of the inside out functional uncertainty expression ((ADJUNCTS $\uparrow$) LCS). This introduces a potential problem, since there is no guarantee that the solution chosen for this functional uncertainty expression is the same each time. It is quite possible that no harm will result (since at least in this simple case, it seems that substituting in different solutions to the functional uncertainty expression will not allow a meaning to be derived for the whole sentence). But since we will now want to refer to this higher feature structure even more times, it seems safest to accurately encode the intention that we wish to refer to the same feature structure each time. So we will use a feature equation with a feature structure variable f to achieve this. Note that this equation is a feature equation, and not a glue language expression.

Here is the formulation we suggest:

(29) **a contracor**   (ADJUNCTS $\uparrow$) $= f$
    AdvP   (f TERMS.1) $\rightsquigarrow X \multimap$
                  (f TERMS.1) $\rightsquigarrow X \otimes$
                  ((f LCS) $\rightsquigarrow Y \multimap$ (f LCS) $\rightsquigarrow unwillingly(X, Y)$)

The feature equation in (29) will pick out one of the feature-structures to which the adverbial phrase bears the ADJUNCTS relation. Given the sharing of ρ between the two levels of the complex predicate structure, this can be either the Cause or the Effect α-structure. The linear logic expression will yield a consequent that operates on the meaning of this structure to produce a revised meaning which incorporates the meaning of the adverbial. In this way, an adverb in a Romance complex predicate will be able to scope at any level within the complex predicate. This seems to be the normal result for monoclausal complex predicates. Dalrymple et al. (1995a:4) note a corresponding ambiguity for complex predicate in Urdu, observed by Butt (1993), and Manning et al. (in press) discuss similar data in Japanese.

In this section we have shown how our proposals for differential information spreading can combine quite straightforwardly with the glue-language semantics approach of DLPS. In particular, we would argue that our approach to argument structure through the use of a TERMS list solve certain problems and inelegancies within the work of DLPS, and in particular, the more articulated feature structures we employ allows one to capture the result that complex predicates 'respect the tree structure', whereas this result is not capture in Dalrymple et al.'s own work, as is discussed further in Appendix B.

B

Previous Proposals

In this appendix we briefly examine three formal proposals for the treatment of complex predicates. These proposals have all been mainly concerned with formal and technical issues, and have not been further applied to a substantial range of empirical data. The first deals with complex predicates on a semantic projection by using the traditional projection architecture of LFG. The second is based on some proposals by Kaplan and Wedekind to build semantic interpretations by means of a restriction concept. The third uses glue-logic semantics to do the work of linking.

All three of these proposals centre around providing an analysis for the Urdu Permissive, a construction which we have already discussed in Chapter 2 above, and re-illustrate here for convenience:

(1) Anjum ne   diyaa Saddaf ko   xat   lik^h-ne
    Anjum ERG gave Saddaf DAT letter.NOM write-INF
    'Anjum let Saddaf write a letter.'

As we have already discussed, scrambling data suggests these permissives have two possible c-structures, one in which **xat lik^{h}ne** is a constituent, and another in which **lik^{h}ne diyaa** is a constituent. There is ample evidence that this construction has a 'flat' f-structure of the form indicated in (a) below, and all the work discussed here assumes in common with us a more articulated semantic structure. For this appendix, we will represent it using Kaplan and Wedekind's (1993) notational conventions as (b). The attributes of the semantic structure σ include REL for predicates, and ARG1, ARG2, etc. for the arguments, giving a straightforward encoding of a predicate-calculus-like logical notation.

(2) a. $\begin{bmatrix} \text{PRED} & \text{x-write}\langle \text{SUBJ, OBJ, OBJ2}\rangle \\ \text{SUBJ} & \text{Anjum} \\ \text{OBJ2} & \text{Saddaf} \\ \text{OBJ} & \text{letter} \end{bmatrix}$

b.
$$
\begin{bmatrix}
\text{REL} & \text{let} \\
\text{ARG1} & \text{Anjum} \\
\text{ARG2} & [\text{Saddaf}] \\
\text{ARG3} & \begin{bmatrix} \text{REL} & \text{write} \\ \text{ARG1} & [\ ] \\ \text{ARG2} & \text{letter} \end{bmatrix}
\end{bmatrix}
$$

1 Projection architectures

Traditionally LFG has assumed a projection architecture where there are multiple distinct levels of representation related by partial correspondence functions. Within this conception, levels of argument structure and semantics can be handled by augmenting the traditional model of a correspondence ϕ between c-structure and f-structure with new levels and new correspondence between them (Kaplan 1995:23). In particular, this section considers whether the Urdu Permissive can be satisfactorily dealt with by adding a semantic projection σ, and answers this question negatively.

The standard conception has the semantic projection coming off the f-structure, corresponding to the idea that f-structures are an intermediate level used in determining predicate-argument structure, and hence meaning. But it is difficult to see how the Urdu Permissive can be accommodated at all in an approach that views σ-structure as a projection off f-structure, similar in nature to ϕ. For in this case we have to transform a flat f-structure back into a multipredicate σ-structure. Such a mapping is impossible to do in a straightforward way, because σ is a function and so the f-structure corresponding to both verbs and the sentence as a whole must have a single σ-structure correspondent. We need to propose something much more elaborate, as in Kaplan and Wedekind (1993), discussed below.

An alternative analysis via projections is one where f-structure and σ-structure are both projections off c-structure, with the two being related via composite functions through c-structure nodes, such as $\phi' = \sigma^{-1} \circ \phi$ and $\sigma' = \phi^{-1} \circ \sigma$ (Halvorsen and Kaplan 1988, Butt et al. 1990). This alternative is also inadequate (this observation is due to John Maxwell (p.c., 1992)). Consider what happens if we embed sentence (1) as the sentential complement of *I believe* .... We would want to do this via a c-structure rule of the form:

(3) S $\rightarrow$ ...   S'   ...
    ($\uparrow$ COMP) = $\downarrow$

and specify the relation between the syntax and the semantics of the object of belief lexically via a rule on the verb such as:[1]

(4) $(\uparrow_\sigma \text{ ARG2}) = (\uparrow_\phi \text{ COMP})_{\phi^{-1}\sigma}$

The equation says that the ARG2 of the matrix verb is the σ-structure of the c-structure node that produced the COMP. But, unfortunately, in this case two c-structure nodes contribute to the COMP (as the complex predicate is monoclausal at f-structure) and they have different σ-structures, as shown in (5).

(5)

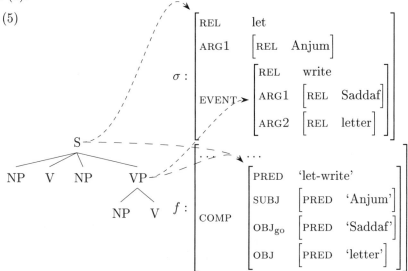

From the COMP's value, ϕ^{-1} takes one back to both the S and the VP node and then the σ correspondence takes one to both the outer and inner clause of the σ-structure. ϕ^{-1} is not a function. We want the semantic value of the COMP to be that of the outer σ-structure shown above, but this approach does not allow us to get at it uniquely. And an approach that tried to project f-structure off σ-structure would suffer from exactly the same problem. The flatness of the f-structure creates problems for a simple projection architecture, no matter how the different projections are arranged.

---

[1]We would not wish to mention the ARG2 in the phrase structure rule, because then the correspondence between ARG2 and a certain phrase structural position would be fixed, whereas we want it to be able to vary according to the verb (i.e., to have the relationship mediated by grammatical relations in the usual way).

2 Kaplan and Wedekind's restrictions proposal

Kaplan and Wedekind (1993) (henceforth KW) propose an analysis of complex predicates in Urdu utilizing the original concept of restriction in LFG, which we presented as 'negative restriction' in Chapter 1 above. KW wish to maintain the standard conception of a semantic projection σ coming directly off of the f-structure. The basic idea of how to maintain that architecture and yet get things to work out is that the lexical entry of the light verb takes as its event argument the semantic correspondent of a structure formed by 'restricting off' the SUBJ GF, which supplies the additional argument supplied by the causative light verb. The substructure that is the value of ARG3 of σ is produced by 'restricting off' the SUBJ-value from the f-structure of the matrix S, that is, using the (negative) restriction operator to produce a new f-structure that is just like that of the S except that it has no SUBJ-attribute. This semantic structure can be produced by having the lexical entry of the light verb **diyaa** 'give' produce an appropriate REL-value and assign arguments to semantic roles as indicated by the following equations:[2]

(6)   *diyaa*   V $(\uparrow_\sigma \text{ REL}) = \text{let}$
                          $(\uparrow_\sigma \text{ ARG1}) = (\uparrow \text{ SUBJ})_\sigma$
                          $(\uparrow_\sigma \text{ ARG2}) = (\uparrow_\sigma \text{ ARG3 ARG1})$
                          $(\uparrow_\sigma \text{ ARG3}) = (\uparrow\backslash\text{SUBJ})_\sigma$

The heavy verb **lik^{h}ne** is then provided by lexical rule with two lexical entries, one for its ordinary main-clause use, the second for its use as pseudo-complement of a light verb. The main version associates SUBJ and OBJ with ARG1 and ARG2 of the REL 'write', while the pseudo-complement version does this with OBJ2 and OBJ, and also places the semantic material in a semantic projection of the f-structure restricted by SUBJ:[3]

---

[2]The presentation below is partly based on the unpublished handout Kaplan and Wedekind (1992), since Kaplan and Wedekind (1993) is not fully explicit about some of the details of the analysis.

[3] In Kaplan and Wedekind (1992), the pseudo-complement entry had the additional equation $((\uparrow\backslash\text{SUBJ}) \text{ PRED}) = \text{'write}\langle\text{OBJ2, OBJ}\rangle\text{'}$, but this PRED-attribute has no clear function, and furthermore clashes with the other introduced PRED-value, so is omitted here.

(7) $lik^h ne$ V main:

$(\uparrow \text{PRED}) = \text{'write}\langle\text{SUBJ, OBJ}\rangle\text{'}$

$(\uparrow_\sigma \text{REL}) = \text{write}$

$(\uparrow_\sigma \text{ARG1}) = (\uparrow \text{SUBJ})_\sigma$

$(\uparrow_\sigma \text{ARG2}) = (\uparrow \text{OBJ})_\sigma$

pseudo-complement:

$(\uparrow \text{PRED}) = \text{'x-write}\langle\text{SUBJ, OBJ2, OBJ}\rangle\text{'}$

$((\uparrow\backslash\text{SUBJ})_\sigma \text{REL}) = \text{write}$

$((\uparrow\backslash\text{SUBJ})_\sigma \text{ARG1}) = (\uparrow \text{OBJ2})_\sigma$

$((\uparrow\backslash\text{SUBJ})_\sigma \text{ARG2}) = (\uparrow \text{OBJ})_\sigma$

The pseudo-complement entry will have the effect of linking the OBJ2 and OBJ functions to the ARG1 and ARG2 of the semantic projection of the sentence's f-structure restricted by SUBJ, but this is the same thing as the ARG3-value of the semantic projection of the sentence's f-structure, which delivers (2b).

The restriction operator thus allows us to derive an f-structure from the f-structure correspondent of some node, and provide it with a semantic projection, thereby in a sense 'unflattening it'. The dual lexical entries for the main verbs can furthermore be produced by a lexical rule which replaces references to SUBJ with references to OBJ2, and references to $\uparrow_\sigma$ with references to $(\uparrow\backslash\text{SUBJ})_\sigma$, thereby deriving the semantic projection equations of the pseudo-complement entry automatically from those of the main entry for verbs like **lik^{h}ne**.

Unexplained on this account is the change in the PRED-attribute; in fact it is unclear to us that the PRED-attribute is actually doing anything in the analysis, suggesting that the role of PRED in this architecture ought to be reconsidered.[4]

Excepting the PRED-problem, this analysis seems to work for this particular case in Urdu, but fails to generalize to other forms of complex predicates in at least two ways, both involving the possibility of recursive application of complex predicate formation.

The first involves the cases, which we have frequently discussed above, where multiple light verbs appear in a 'stack'. An Italian example from Rizzi (1982) is presented in (8) below, while (9) is a Spanish equivalent from Manning (1992):

(8) a. Maria avrebbe voluto andare a prender-**li** lei stessa
       'Maria would have (**avere**) wanted to go to get them herself.'
    b. Maria **li** avrebbe voluti andare a prendere lei stessa

---

[4]And, indeed, the handout Kaplan and Wedekind (1992) also suggests this and proposes one possible new approach.

(9) a. quiero tratar de terminar de mostrar-**te-lo** mañana
        'I want to try to finish showing them to you tomorrow.'
     b. **te lo** quiero tratar de terminar de mostrar mañana

The climbing of the clitics indicates that the (b) examples have light verbs, which are appearing in a c-structure ordering reflecting their semantic scope.

An initial difficulty in extending the analysis of Urdu Permissives to these constructions is that they do not add an argument, so we cannot build the f-structure to produce the pseudo-complement semantic structures simply by restricting off some grammatical function. But this problem can be met by adapting the devices used in the analysis that Kaplan and Wedekind (1992, 1993) propose for adverbs.

Adverbs are taken to introduce their f-structures as members of a set-valued attribute such as ADJ(UNCTS) or MODS. The semantic interpretation of structures containing such an attribute is then provided by a rule that applies recursively, from the top down, in effect taking some adverb from the adjunct-pool and setting it as the semantic head, and taking as argument whatever is then found to be the semantic projection of the resulting reduced f-structure. This is achieved with the help of an extension of the concept of restriction which defines the result of removing a member a from a set-valued attribute g. This extended concept of restriction can be defined as follows:

$$(10) \quad f\backslash\langle a\ g\rangle \equiv_{def} \begin{cases} f\backslash a & \text{if } (fa) - \{g\} = \emptyset \\[2mm] f\backslash a \cup \{\langle a, (fa) - \{g\}\rangle\} & \text{otherwise} \end{cases}$$

The effect of this definition is to allow the members of a set to be successively removed, and then the interpretation of each f-structure can be made to depend on that of the results of the removal of something from it.

Now suppose that the non-argument-adding light verbs each add an element to a set-valued attribute which we will call MODALS. Then the Italian example above would have an f-structure like this:

$$(11) \quad \begin{bmatrix} \text{SUBJ} & \begin{bmatrix} \text{PRED} & \text{'Maria'} \end{bmatrix} \\[2mm] \text{MODALS} & \left\{ \begin{bmatrix} \text{PRED} & \text{'Perf'} \end{bmatrix} \begin{bmatrix} \text{PRED} & \text{'Able'} \end{bmatrix} \begin{bmatrix} \text{PRED} & \text{'About-}^{\text{to}'} \end{bmatrix} \right\} \\[2mm] \text{PRED} & \text{'Get}\langle\text{SUBJ, OBJ}\rangle\text{'} \\[2mm] \text{ADJUNCTS} & \{ \textit{herself} \} \end{bmatrix}$$

We can now provide for the semantic interpretation of such structures by means of the following adaptation of the adverb rule in Kaplan and Wedekind (1992), which is supposed to apply in a nondeterministic fashion:[5]

(12) If f is an f-structure and $g \in (f \text{ MODALS})$, then
$$f_\sigma = g_\sigma \text{ and } (f_\sigma \text{ ARG1}) = (f \backslash \langle \text{MODS } g \rangle)_\sigma$$

This rule produces its effects by interacting with appropriate lexical entries. Here is an entry for the 'Perf' light-verb form **avrebbe**:

(13)   *avrebbe*   V $(\uparrow \text{PRED}) = $ 'Perf'
$(\uparrow_\sigma \text{REL}) = \text{perfect}$

Initially, the semantic projection of the light verb will correspond to the member f-structure within the MODALS-value. But rule (12) can apply and set this semantic projection to also be the semantic projection of the entire f-structure. Then the ARG1-value of this semantic projection is computed by removing this light-verb from the MODALS set, and finding the semantic projection of the result. Eventually all of the elements of the MODALS attribute will disappear, and therefore, by the first clause of (10) the MODALS attribute itself will disappear. Then we need to find the semantic projection of what is left.

This can be done by revising the lexical entries for ordinary main verbs so that they provide a semantic projection for their f-structure with MODALS restricted off:

(14)   *prendere*   V $(\uparrow \text{PRED}) = $ 'Prendere$\langle \text{SUBJ, OBJ} \rangle$'
$((\uparrow \backslash \text{MODALS})_\sigma \text{ REL}) = \text{take}$
. . .

This analysis will produce a nested semantic structure from a flat c-structure,[6] but suffers from the important defect that it does not provide any explanation for the fact that the semantic scope of the light verbs reflects their order of nesting in the c-structure. Because the rule (12) applies nondeterministically, it can interpret the light verbs in any order at all, regardless of their c-structure arrangement. The fact that the interpretation 'respects the tree' therefore goes unexplained.

Another and worse form of this problem arises in connection with Alsina's Catalan examples of respecting the tree, previously mentioned, but repeated below for convenience, in which an aspectual light verb appears either inside or outside of the scope of a causative.

---

[5]Note that because this rule is supposed to be part of UG, its complexity is not a strong argument against it.

[6]Although there are various further details to be attended to. For example, the ability verb form **potuto** seems to ascribe a semantic role to the SUBJ. This is not provided for in the analysis given.

(15) a. Li   acabo de fer   llegir la carta
        Him.DAT I.finish of make read the map
        'I finish making him read the map.'
    b. Li   faig   acabar de llegir la   carta
        Him.DAT I.make finish of read the map
        'I make him finish reading the map.'

It is quite unclear to us how to integrate a Kaplan and Wedekind-style analysis of the causative here with an adverbial-style or any other kind of analysis of the aspectual verb, let alone in such a way as to cause the tree-structure to determine the scope.

The second kind of problem arises with multiple causatives, such as this French one from Kayne (1975:261):[7]

(16) Elle lui   a   fait   laisser tomber ses bouquins
    She him.DAT has made let   fall   his books
    'She made him let his books fall.'

Here the main verb is intransitive, so we will somehow need to elaborate the lexical rule for pseudo-complement main verbs so that it can convert the SUBJ in an intransitive into an OBJ for a single causative, and then provide for converting this new SUBJ into an OBJ2 in the doubly causativized from, as well as respecting the tree in the semantic interpretation (*let cause* versus for example *cause let*). Again, it is quite unclear to us how any of this is to be achieved in a manner that is explanatory and supports simple descriptions.

It does not follow from this discussion that KW's proposal is definitely wrong and should be abandoned, but it clearly needs much more work before becoming an empirically serious contender.

3   A resource logic proposal

In this section we examine a proposal by Dalrymple et al. (1995a) (henceforth DHLS) to analyse complex predicates by means of the 'glue-language semantics' already presented in Appendix A. Like KW, DHLS analyse Urdu permissive causatives, and the treatment faces the same problem of apparent failure to generalize to a wider range of constructions.

To analyse light verbs, DHLS introduce a significant change in how the meanings of arguments are supplied to the meaning of predicates. In the exposition of DLPS above, the meaning-constructors of verbs accessed the meanings of arguments via direct mention of grammatical relations. In the DHLS approach, verbal meaning-constructors access argument meanings by means of thematic-relation labels which are taken as constituting a level

---

[7]Such sentences are accepted by most but not all speakers, according to Kayne, who marks them with a '?'.

of 'argument-structure'. There is then a set of 'linking rules', formulated as linear logic deductive principles, which build the argument-structure by transferring argument meanings from the grammatical relation values to the argument-structure.

For the verb **lik^{h}aa** 'write', DHLS propose the following meaning-constructor:

(17) $lik^h aa$ V $(\uparrow \text{PRED}) = \text{'Write'}$
$$\forall X, Y.(\uparrow_\sigma \text{AGENT}) \rightsquigarrow X \otimes (\uparrow_\sigma \text{THEME}) \rightsquigarrow Y \multimap$$
$$\uparrow_\sigma \rightsquigarrow write(X,Y)$$

For a sentence such as:

(18)   Saddaf-ne   xat   lik^{h}aa
     Saddaf-ERG letter write
     'Saddaf wrote a/the letter.'

We will now get f-structure and semantic information as follows:

(19)
$$f: \begin{bmatrix} \text{SUBJ} & g: \begin{bmatrix} \text{PRED} & \text{'Anjum'} \end{bmatrix} \text{---} \\ \text{PRED} & \text{'Write'} \\ \text{OBJ} & h: \begin{bmatrix} \text{PRED} & \text{'letter'} \end{bmatrix} \text{--} \end{bmatrix} \begin{matrix} \text{- - - -} \blacktriangleright j \\ \text{- - - -} \blacktriangleright i \\ \text{- - - -} \blacktriangleright k \end{matrix}$$

$\forall X, Y.(i \text{ AGENT}) \rightsquigarrow X \otimes (i \text{ THEME}) \rightsquigarrow Y \multimap i \rightsquigarrow write(X,Y)$
$j \rightsquigarrow Anjum$
$k \rightsquigarrow letter$

But as it stands we cannot do much with these assertions, since the argument-meanings are connected to grammatical relations values, and the antecedent conjuncts of the predicate-meaning refer to thematic relation values. To bridge this gap, DHLS employ a part of linear logic that has not been mentioned, yet, 'standing assertions' that can be utilized without being consumed. These are notated by prefixing them with a '!' (read 'bang') operator; the principle proposed by DHLS is:

(20) $!(\forall F, X, Y.((F \text{ SUBJ})_\sigma \rightsquigarrow X) \otimes ((F \text{ OBJ})_\sigma \rightsquigarrow Y) \multimap$
$$((F_\sigma \text{ AGENT}) \rightsquigarrow X) \otimes ((F_\sigma \text{ THEME}) \rightsquigarrow Y)$$

Combining this assertion and the second and third premises in (19) allows us to replace the meaning-constructors of (19) with:

(21) $^i\begin{bmatrix} \text{AGENT} & [\,] \rightsquigarrow Anjum \\ \text{THEME} & [\,] \rightsquigarrow letter \end{bmatrix}$
$\forall X, Y.(i \text{ AGENT}) \rightsquigarrow X \otimes (i \text{ THEME}) \rightsquigarrow Y \multimap i \rightsquigarrow write(X,Y)$

Observe that the mapping has actually created some structure on the semantic projection, in the form of placeholders for the subject and object meanings. We have written the meaning-constructors into the structure rather than utilizing additional italic variables to represent them. This is a notation we will use further below. Such structure-creation also plays an important role in the analysis of quantification in (Dalrymple et al. 1997).

Now the meaning-constructor provided by the verb can apply, and yield an assertion ascribing a meaning to the sentence's entire f-structure:

(22) $i \leadsto Write(Anjum, letter)$

With the use of mapping rules, we can provide an analysis of Urdu permissive causatives along the following lines. The light verb **diyaa** will have a meaning constructor that consumes a 'permitter' thematic role and an 'ordinary' sentence meaning to produce a causativized meaning:

(23) $diyaa$ V $\forall X, P.((\uparrow_\sigma \text{ PERMITTER}) \leadsto X) \otimes (\uparrow_\sigma \leadsto P) \multimap$
      $\uparrow_\sigma \leadsto permit(X, P)$

The f-structure and semantic structure for the permissive causative sentence will now look like this,[8] where we have written several of the meaning-constructors into the feature-structure rather than using the italic variables:

(24)
$$
f: \begin{bmatrix} \text{SUBJ} & g:\begin{bmatrix} \text{PRED} & \text{`Anjum'} \end{bmatrix} \text{-} \\ \text{PRED} & \text{`write'} \\ \text{OBJ} & h:\begin{bmatrix} \text{PRED} & \text{`Letter'} \end{bmatrix}\text{-} \\ \text{OBJ2} & i:\begin{bmatrix} \text{PRED} & \text{`Saddaf'} \end{bmatrix}\text{-} \end{bmatrix}
\begin{array}{l} \dashrightarrow [\ ] \leadsto Anjum \\ \dashrightarrow [\ ] \\ \dashrightarrow [\ ] \leadsto letter \\ \dashrightarrow [\ ] \leadsto Saddaf \end{array}
$$

$\forall X, Y.(f_\sigma \text{ AGENT}) \leadsto X \otimes (f_\sigma \text{ THEME}) \leadsto Y \multimap f_\sigma \leadsto write(X, Y)$
$\forall X, P.((f_\sigma \text{ PERMITTER}) \leadsto X) \otimes (f_\sigma \leadsto P) \multimap f_\sigma \leadsto permit(X, P)$

Our current mapping rule would clearly be quite inappropriate for mapping from the grammatical relations to the thematic roles in this example, so we need a new one:

(25) $!(\forall F, X, Y, Z.(F \text{ SUBJ})_\sigma \leadsto X \otimes (F \text{ OBJ})_\sigma \leadsto Y \otimes (F \text{ OBJ2})_\sigma \leadsto Z \multimap$
      $(F_\sigma \text{ PERMITTER}) \leadsto X \otimes (F_\sigma \text{ AGENT}) \leadsto Y \otimes (F_\sigma \text{ THEME}) \leadsto Z$

This will remove the meanings from the σ-projections of the various noun-phrases, and will provide us with the following semantic information for the f-structure f:

---

[8]In the text of DHLS, example (24), the PRED-value is actually specified as 'PER-MIT(WRITE)', with no account of how this value is actually to be produced. We suspect that this lacuna reflects unclarity as to what the PRED-attribute is actually supposed to be doing in the analysis.

(26)
$$f_\sigma : \begin{bmatrix} \text{PERMITTER} & [\,]\rightsquigarrow Anjum \\ \text{AGENT} & [\,]\rightsquigarrow Saddaf \\ \text{THEME} & [\,]\rightsquigarrow Letter \end{bmatrix}$$

$$\forall X, Y.(f_\sigma \text{ AGENT}) \rightsquigarrow X \otimes (f_\sigma \text{ THEME}) \rightsquigarrow Y \multimap f_\sigma \rightsquigarrow write(X, Y)$$
$$\forall X, P.((f_\sigma \text{ PERMITTER}) \rightsquigarrow X) \otimes (f_\sigma \rightsquigarrow P) \multimap f_\sigma \rightsquigarrow permit(X, P)$$

Now the 'write' meaning-constructor can be used in order to produce (27) from (26):

(27)
$$f_\sigma : \begin{bmatrix} \text{PERMITTER} & [\,]\rightsquigarrow Anjum \\ \text{AGENT} & [\,] \\ \text{THEME} & [\,] \end{bmatrix}\rightsquigarrow write(Saddaf, Letter)$$

$$\forall X, P.((f_\sigma \text{ PERMITTER}) \rightsquigarrow X) \otimes (f_\sigma \rightsquigarrow P) \multimap f_\sigma \rightsquigarrow permit(X, P)$$

(27) provides a meaning for the f-structure of the sentence, but it hasn't used all the meaning-constructors it started out with, so it does not specify the meaning for the sentence. To finish up, we use the 'permit' meaning-constructor to go from (27) to:

(28)
$$f_\sigma : \begin{bmatrix} \text{PERMITTER} & [\,] \\ \text{AGENT} & [\,] \\ \text{THEME} & [\,] \end{bmatrix}\rightsquigarrow permit(Anjum, write(Saddaf, Letter))$$

This account works rather more smoothly than Kaplan and Wedekind's, in part because the availability of linking rules makes it possible to dispense with the lexical rules. But it still faces similar problems. In the first place, it does not provide any reason for the semantic scoping of multiple light verbs to reflect their relative positions in the tree. Suppose we accept a simple one-place predicate interpretation for a light verb such as Catalan **acabar** 'finish'. This verb could then introduce the following meaning-constructor:

(29) $\forall P.\uparrow_\sigma \rightsquigarrow P \multimap \uparrow_\sigma \rightsquigarrow finish(P)$

Alsina's oft-repeated examples:

(30) a. Li   acabo de fer   llegir la   carta
       Him.DAT I.finish of make read the map
       'I finish making him read the map.'

    b. Li   faig   acabar de llegir la   carta
       Him.DAT I.make finish   of   read the map
       'I make him finish reading the map.'

can then get meanings such as:

(31) a. $cause(I, finish(read(he, map)))$

b. $finish(cause(I, read(he, map)))$

But there is a problem; each of the two examples will be able to get either of the two readings, since if the analysis of these examples is carried out the the same general way as that of Urdu, both of the examples will provide the following collection of meaning-constructors ready to provide a meaning for the top-level f-structure f:

(32)
$$f_\sigma: \begin{bmatrix} \text{CAUSER} & [\,] \rightsquigarrow I \\ \text{AGENT} & [\,] \rightsquigarrow he \\ \text{THEME} & [\,] \rightsquigarrow map \end{bmatrix}$$

$\forall X, Y.(f_\sigma \text{ AGENT}) \rightsquigarrow X \otimes (f_\sigma \text{ THEME}) \rightsquigarrow Y \multimap f_\sigma \rightsquigarrow read(X, Y)$
$\forall X, P.((f_\sigma \text{ PERMITTER}) \rightsquigarrow X) \otimes (f_\sigma \rightsquigarrow P) \multimap f_\sigma \rightsquigarrow cause(X, P)$
$\forall P.f_\sigma \rightsquigarrow P \multimap f_\sigma \rightsquigarrow finish(P)$

The heavy verb's constructor can then dispose of the meanings of the AGENT and THEME-values, yielding:

(33)
$$f_\sigma: \begin{bmatrix} \text{CAUSER} & [\,] \rightsquigarrow I \\ \text{AGENT} & [\,] \\ \text{THEME} & [\,] \end{bmatrix} \rightsquigarrow read(he, map)$$

$\forall X, P.((f_\sigma \text{ CAUSER}) \rightsquigarrow X) \otimes (f_\sigma \rightsquigarrow P) \multimap f_\sigma \rightsquigarrow cause(X, P)$
$\forall P.f_\sigma \rightsquigarrow P \multimap f_\sigma \rightsquigarrow finish(P)$

The problem is that now the 'cause' and 'finish' meaning-constructors can be applied in either order, producing either of the readings of (31).

A further problem with this analysis follows from the way in which it uses thematic role labels. In general the proposed linking theory is quite ad hoc, and makes no attempt to do more than stipulate rules for analysing the two sentences at hand. But the main issue is that, as the analysis is currently conceived, each argument of a verb must have a unique thematic role, which is preserved under valence-changing operations, so that the heavy verb can find its arguments regardless of whatever light-verb environment it may be put into. So an additional argument, such as one introduced by a causative, needs a new label, such as PERMITTER or CAUSER. Not only is this quite nonstandard, but it creates clear difficulties because these additional arguments have various properties in common with AGENTS, which therefore cannot be described without loss of generalizations.

Consider for example the case of light verbs with meanings such as 'want', which ascribe a semantic role to one of the arguments of the heavy verb. Such a verb could be plausibly given a meaning-constructor like this (note the 'premise copying', for the same reason as in our analysis of causatives in Appendix A):

(34) $\forall X, P.(\uparrow_\sigma \text{ AGENT}) \rightsquigarrow X \multimap$
$\qquad (\uparrow_\sigma \rightsquigarrow P \multimap \uparrow_\sigma \rightsquigarrow want(X, P)) \otimes$
$\qquad (\uparrow_\sigma \text{ AGENT}) \rightsquigarrow X$

Such light verbs can be applied either to simple heavy verbs, or to causative constructions consisting of a light and a heavy verb, as in these Italian examples:

(35) a. lo voglio mangiare
   it I-want to-eat
   'I want to eata it.'

  b. lo voglio far mangiare
   it I-want to-make to-eat
   'I want to make him eat it.'

We need to identify the WANTER of **voglio** with the AGENT of **mangiare**, but the PERMITTER of **far**, but since the thematic roles are atomic labels, the only way to this is stipulatively, missing the generalization that it is the top term on the argument-list of the pseudo-complement material that gets identified as the WANTER of **voglio**.

As with the KW proposal, there might be solutions to the problems with this approach, but they are not entirely obvious. The proposal would need a great deal more development to be a serious theory of complex predicates.

Bibliography

Abeillé, Anne, and Danièle Godard. 1994. The complementation of tense auxiliaries in French. In *The Proceedings of the Thirteenth West Coast Conference on Formal Linguistics*, ed. Raul Aranovich, William Byrne, Susanne Preuss, and Martha Senturia, 157–172. Stanford, CA. Stanford Linguistics Association. [60–61]

Abeillé, Anne, and Danièle Godard. 1996. La Complémentation des Auxiliaires Français. *Langages* 122:32–61. [61]

Abeillé, Anne, Danièle Godard, and Ivan A. Sag. in press. Two Kinds of Composition in French Complex Predicates. In *Complex Predicates in non-derivational syntax*, ed. Andreas Kathol, Erhard Hinrichs, and Tsuneko Nakazawa. New York: Academic Press. [59]

Abney, Stephen P. 1987. *The English Noun Phrase in its Sentential Aspect.* Doctoral dissertation, MIT. [2, 6]

Ackerman, Farrell, and Phil LeSourd. 1997. Toward a lexical representation of phrasal predicates. In Alex Alsina, Joan Bresnan, and Peter Sells, eds. 67–106. [5, 19]

Ackerman, Farrell, and Gert Webelhuth. 1996. The Construct PREDICATE: Empirical arguments and theoretical status. In *Proceedings of the First LFG Conference (LFG-96)*, ed. Miriam Butt and Tracy Holloway King. Rank Xerox, Grenoble. http://www-csli.stanford.edu/publications/LFG/lfg1.html. [19]

Aikhenvald, Alexandra Y. 1994. Grammatical Relations in Tariana. *Nordic Journal of Linguistics* 17:201–217. [71–72]

Aikhenvald, Alexandra Y. 1995. Serial Verb Constructions and Verb-Compounding in Tariana. Paper presented at SSILA Annual Meeting, Alberquerque NM; MS, Australian National University. [72, 75]

Aikhenvald, Alexandra Y. to appear a. Reciprocal and sociative in Tariana: their genetic and areal properties. In *The Typology of Reciprocals*, ed. V.P. Nedialkov. Munich: Lingcom Europa. [80]

Aikhenvald, Alexandra Y. to appear b. Transitivity in Tariana. In *Transitivity: Devices and Designs.* [2, 71, 73, 75, 89]

Aissen, Judith, and David M. Perlmutter. 1976. Clause Reduction in Spanish.

In *Papers from the Second Annual Meeting of the Berkely Linguistic Society*. 1–30. [9, 27]

Aissen, Judith, and David M. Perlmutter. 1983. Clause Reduction in Spanish. In *Studies in Relational Grammar I*, ed. David M. Permutter. 360–403. Chicago: University of Chicago Press. [27, 53]

Alsina, Alex. 1993. *Predicate Composition: A Theory of Syntactic Function Alternations*. Doctoral dissertation, Stanford University. [10, 19, 26, 64]

Alsina, Alex. 1996. *The Role of Argument Structure in Grammar*. Stanford, CA: CSLI Publications. [4, 6, 16, 19, 26, 39–40, 45, 51, 55, 59]

Alsina, Alex. 1997. A Theory of Complex Predicates: Evidence from Causatives in Bantu and Romance. In Alex Alsina, Joan Bresnan, and Peter Sells, eds. 203–246. [9, 19, 26, 29–30, 35, 39–41, 45, 78]

Alsina, Alex, Joan Bresnan, and Peter Sells (eds.). 1997. *Complex Predicates*. Stanford, CA: CSLI Publications. [2, 9]

Alsina, Alex, and Smita Joshi. 1991. Parameters in Causative Constructions. In *Papers from the 27th Regional Meeting of the Chicago Linguistics Society*, ed. Lise M. Dobrin, Lynn Nichols, and Rosa M. Rodriguez, Vol. 1, 1–15. [19, 45]

Andrews, Avery. 1983. A Note on the Constituent Structure of Modifiers. *Linguistic Inquiry* 14:695–7. [7]

Andrews, Avery. 1985. The Major Functions of the Noun Phrase. In *Language Typology and Syntactic Description, vol 1: Clause Structure*, ed. Tim Shopen. Cambridge University Press. [72]

Andrews, Avery D. 1990. Case-Structures and Control in Modern Icelandic. In *Modern Icelandic Syntax*, ed. Joan Maling and Annie Zaenen. 187–234. Academic Press. [88]

Andrews, Avery D., and Christopher D. Manning. 1993. Information-Spreading and Levels of Representation in LFG. Technical Report CSLI-93-176. Stanford, CA: CSLI, Stanford University. Available at: http://www.sultry.arts.usyd.edu.au/cmanning/papers. [58–59, 107]

Baker, Mark. 1989. Object-Sharing and Projection in Serial Verb Constructions. *Linguistic Inquiry* 20:513–553. [71, 103–104, 107–108]

Baker, Mark C. 1988. *Incorporation: A Theory of Grammatical Function Changing*. Chicago, IL: University of Chicago press. [45, 115–116]

Bittner, Maria. 1997. Concealed Causatives. Rutgers ms. [91, 94, 100]

Bodomo, Adams B. 1996. Complex verbal predicates: the case of serial verbs in Dagaare and Akan. In *Proceedings of the First LFG Conference (LFG-96)*, ed. Miriam Butt and Tracy Holloway King. Rank Xerox, Grenoble. http://www-csli.stanford.edu/publications/LFG/lfg1.html. [76]

Bodomo, Adams B. 1997. *Paths and Pathfinders: Exploring the Syntax and Semantics of Complex Verbal Predicates in Dagaare and Other Languages*. Doctoral dissertation, Norwegian University of Science and Technology, Trondeim, Norway. [103, 105, 110–111]

Bresnan, Joan W. (ed.). 1982. *The Mental Representation of Grammatical Relations*. Cambridge, MA: MIT Press. [1–2]

Bresnan, Joan W. 1997. Mixed Categories as Head-Sharing Constructions. In *Proceedings of the Second LFG Conference (LFG-97)*, ed. Miriam Butt and Tracy Holloway King. University of California, San Diego. http://www-csli.stanford.edu/publications/LFG2/lfg97.html. [22]

Bresnan, Joan W. in prep. *Lexical-Functional Syntax*. Blackwell. MS, Stanford University. [4, 6]

Bresnan, Joan W., and Jonni M. Kanerva. 1989. Locative Inversion in Chicheŵa: a Case Study of Factorization in Grammar. *Linguistic Inquiry* 20:1–50. [45]

Bresnan, Joan W., and Sam Mchombo. 1987. Topic, Pronoun and Agreement in Chicheŵa. *Language* 63:741–782. Also in Iida, Wechsler and Zec, eds., (1987:1–59). [63]

Bresnan, Joan W., and Annie Zaenen. 1990. Deep Unaccusativity in LFG. In *Proceedings of the Fifth Biennial Conference on Grammatical Relations*, 45–57. University of California, San Diego. [52]

Burzio, Luigi. 1986. *Italian Syntax: a Government-Binding Approach*. Dordrecht: D. Reidel. [27, 52–54, 56]

Butt, Miriam. 1995. *The Structure of Complex Predicates in Urdu*. Stanford, CA: CSLI Publications. [11, 19, 21–25, 33, 43, 59, 90, 108]

Butt, Miriam. 1997. Complex predicates in Urdu. In Alex Alsina, Joan Bresnan, and Peter Sells, eds. 107–149. [19, 24]

Butt, Miriam, Michio Isoda, and Peter Sells. 1990. Complex Predicates in LFG. MS, Stanford University. [11, 33, 130]

Butt, Miriam, María-Eugenia Niño, and Frédérique Segond. 1996. Multilingual Processing of Auxiliaries within LFG. In *Natural Language Processing and Speech Technology*, ed. Dafydd Gibbon. Berlin: Mouton de Gruyter. [32, 46]

Butt, Miriam Jessica. 1993. *The Structure of Complex Predicates in Urdu*. Doctoral dissertation, Stanford. [19, 128]

Carpenter, Bob. 1992. *The Logic of Typed Feature Structures*. Cambridge: Cambridge University Press. [43]

Collins, Chris. 1997. Argument Sharing in Serial Verb Constructions. *Linguistic Inquiry* 28:461–497. [104, 108, 110]

Corbett, Greville G., Norman M. Fraser, and Scott McGlashan (eds.). 1993. *Heads in grammatical theory*. Cambridge: Cambridge University Press. [5, 113]

Crowley, Terry. 1987. Serial Verbs in Paamese. *Studies in Language* 11:35–84. [103, 105]

Dalrymple, Mary, Per-Kristian Halvorsen, Ronald M. Kaplan, Chris Manning, John Maxwell, Jürgen Wedekind, and Annie Zaenen. 1992. Relating projections. MS, Xerox PARC. [33]

Dalrymple, Mary, Angie Hinrichs, John Lamping, and Vijay Saraswat. 1995a. The Resource Logic of Complex Predicate Interpretation. Technical Report ISTL-NLTT-1993-08-03. Palo Alto, CA: Xerox PARC. Revised version of a paper presented at the 1993 Republic of China Computational Linguistics Conference (ROCLING), Hsitou National Park, Taiwan, September 1993. ftp://parcftp.xerox.com/pub/nl/complexpreds.ps. [119, 126, 128, 136]

Dalrymple, Mary, Ronald M. Kaplan, John T. Maxwell, and Annie Zaenen (eds.). 1995b. *Formal Issues in Lexical-Functional Grammar.* Stanford, CA: CSLI Publications.

Dalrymple, Mary, John Lamping, Fernando C. N. Pereira, and Vijay Saraswat. 1997. Quantifiers, Anaphora, and Intensionality. *Journal of Logic, Language and Information* 6:219–273. First available in 1994; obtainable at: ftp://parcftp.xerox.com/pub/nl/quantification.ps. [44, 119–120, 126, 138]

Dalrymple, Mary, John Lamping, and Vijay Saraswat. 1993. LFG Semantics via Constraints. In *Proceedings of the Sixth European ACL.* University of Utrecht. European Chapter of the Association for Computational Linguistics. Available at: ftp://parcftp.xerox.com/pub/nl/eacl93-lfg-sem.ps. [119, 127]

Dalrymple, Mary E. 1993. *The Syntax of Anaphoric Binding.* Stanford, CA: CSLI Publications. [127]

Déchaine, Rose-Marie. 1988. Towards a Typology of Serial Constructions in Haitian. In *Niger-Congo Syntax and Semantics No 1; Papers from the April, 1987 Workshop*, ed. Victor Manfredi, 49–64. Boston University. [105, 109]

Dixon, R.M.W. 1994. *Ergativity.* Cambridge University Press. [72]

Dowty, David. 1991. Thematic Proto-Roles and Argument-Selection. *Language* 67:547–619. [30]

Durie, Mark. 1997. Grammatical Structures in Verb Serialization. In Alex Alsina, Joan Bresnan, and Peter Sells, eds. 289–354. [2, 71, 103–104, 106, 110–111]

Fenstad, Jens Erik, Per-Kristian Halvorsen, Tore Langholm, and Johan van Benthem. 1987. *Situations, Language and Logic.* Dordrecht: D. Reidel. [9]

Fillmore, Charles J., and Paul Kay. in prep. *Construction Grammar.* CSLI Publications. MS, University of California, Berkeley. Available at: http://www.icsi.berkeley.edu/ fillmore/ling220.html. [1]

Foley, William, and Michael Olson. 1985. Clausehood and Verb Serialization. In *Grammar Inside and Outside the Clause*, ed. Joanna Nichols and Anthony C. Woodbury. 17–60. Cambridge University Press. [104, 108, 110]

Foley, William A., and Robert D. Van Valin. 1984. *Functional Syntax and Universal Grammar.* Cambridge University Press. [30, 108]

Frank, Annette. 1996. A Note on Complex Predicate Formation: Evidence from Auxiliary Selection, Reflexivization and Past Participle Agreement in French and Italian. In *Proceedings of the First LFG Conference (LFG-96)*, ed. Miriam Butt and Tracy Holloway King. Rank Xerox, Grenoble. http://www-csli.stanford.edu/publications/LFG/lfg1.html. [32, 59]

Goldberg, Adele. 1995. *Constructions: A Construction Grammar Approach to Argument Structure.* University of Chicago Press. [1]

Grimshaw, Jane. 1990. *Argument Structure.* Cambridge, MA: MIT Press. [52]

Hale, Ken. 1989. The Causative Construction in Miskitu. In *Sentential Complementation and the Lexicon: Studies in Honor of Wim de Geest*, ed. Danny Jasper, Wim Kloster, Yvan Putseys, and Peter Seuren. 189–205. Foris. [91, 95, 97]

Hale, Ken. 1991. Misumalpan Verb Sequencing Constructions. In Claire Lefebvre, ed. [91–92, 110]

Halvorsen, Per-Kristian. 1983. Semantics for Lexical-Functional Grammar. *Linguistic Inquiry* 14:567–615. [9–10]

Halvorsen, Per-Kristian, and Ronald M. Kaplan. 1988. Projections and Semantic Description in Lexical-Functional Grammar. In *Proceedings of the International Conference on Fifth Generation Computer Systems*, 1116–1122. Tokyo. Institute for New Generation Computer Technology. Also published in Dalrymple et. al., eds. 279–292. [11, 130]

Hudson, Richard. 1990. *English Word Grammar*. Basil Blackwell. [2]

Iida, Masayo, Stephen Wechsler, and Draga Zec. 1987. *Working Papers in Discourse and Grammatical Theory*. Stanford, CA: CSLI Publications.

Ishikawa, Akira. 1985. *Complex Predicates and Lexical Operations in Japanese*. Doctoral dissertation, Stanford University. [19, 22]

Jackendoff, Ray S. 1977. *X̄-syntax*. MIT Press. [6]

Jackendoff, Ray S. 1990. *Semantic Structures*. MIT Press. [25, 43]

Johnson, Mark. 1991. Features and Formulae. *Computational Linguisitcs* 17:131–151.

Josefsson, G. 1991. Pseudocoordination: a VP + VP Coordination. *Working Papers in Scandinavian Syntax* 47:130–156. [110]

Kaplan, Ronald M. 1995. The Formal Architecture of LFG. In Mary Dalrymple, Ronald M. Kaplan, John T. Maxwell, and Annie Zaenen, eds. 7–27. [4, 9, 12, 90, 130]

Kaplan, Ronald M., and Joan W. Bresnan. 1982. Lexical-Functional Grammar: a Formal System for Grammatical Representation. In Joan Bresnan, ed. 173–281. Also in Dalrymple, Kaplan, Maxwell and Zaenen, eds. (1995). [4]

Kaplan, Ronald M., and Jügen Wedekind. 1992. Restriction and Structure Misalignment. Handout, Xerox PARC. [132–133, 135]

Kaplan, Ronald M., and Jürgen Wedekind. 1993. Restriction and Correspondence-Based Translation. In *Proceedings of the Sixth European Converence of the Association for Computational Linguistics*. Utrecht. ftp://parcftp.xerox.com/pub/nl/restricton.ps. [13, 129–130, 132]

Kaplan, Ronald M., and Annie Zaenen. 1989. Long-distance Dependencies, Constituent Structure and Functional Uncertainty. In *Alternative Conceptions of Phrase-Structure*, ed. Mark Baltin and Anthony Kroch. 17–42. Chicago: Chicago University Press. Also in Dalrymple, Kaplan, Maxwell and Zaenen, eds. (1995:137–165). [64]

Kathol, Andreas. 1995. *Linearization-based German Syntax*. Doctoral dissertation, Ohio State University. [69]

Kayne, Richard. 1975. *French Syntax*. Cambridge, MA: MIT Press. [26, 64–65, 136]

Kroeger, Paul. 1993. *Phrase-Structure and Grammatical Relations in Tagalog*. Stanford, CA: CSLI Publications. Originally Stanford University PhD disseration, 1991. [6]

Lefebvre, Claire. 1989. Instrumental Take-Serial Constructions in Haitian and in Fon. *Canadian Journal of Linguistics* 34:319–338. [105, 111]

Lefebvre, Claire (ed.). 1991. *Serial Verbs: Grammatical, Comparative and Cognitive Approaches.* John Benjamins. [71, 103]

Lyons, John. 1977. *Semantics.* Cambridge University Press. [2]

Manning, Christopher D. 1992. Romance is so complex. Technical Report CSLI-92-168. Stanford, CA: CSLI, Stanford University. http://www.sultry.arts.usyd.edu.au/cmanning/papers. [10, 39, 55, 126, 133]

Manning, Christopher D. 1996a. *Ergativity: Argument Structure and Grammatical Relations.* Stanford, CA: CSLI Publications. [43, 46, 98]

Manning, Christopher D. 1996b. Romance Complex Predicates: In defence of the right-branching structure. Paper presented at the Workshop on Surfaced-Base Syntax and Romance Languages, 1996 European Summer School on Logic, Language and Information, Prague. Draft available at: http://www.sultry.arts.usyd.edu.au/cmanning/papers. [39, 60]

Manning, Christopher D., and Ivan A. Sag. in press. Argument Structure, Valence, and Binding. *Nordic Journal of Linguistics* 21. [45, 116]

Manning, Christopher D., Ivan A. Sag, and Masayo Iida. in press. The Lexical Integrity of Japanese Causatives. In *Studies in Contemporary Phrase Structure Grammar*, ed. Robert Levine and Georgia Green. Cambridge: Cambridge University Press. http://www.sultry.arts.usyd.edu.au/cmanning/papers. [45, 60, 116, 128]

Marantz, Alec P. 1984. *On the Nature of Grammatical Relations.* Cambridge, MA: MIT Press. [45]

Matsumoto, Yo. 1995. *Complex Predicates in Japanese: A Syntactic and Semantic Study of the Notion 'Word'.* Stanford, CA: CSLI Publications. [84]

Maxwell, III, John T., and Ronald M. Kaplan. 1993. The interface between phrasal and functional constraints. *Computational Linguistics* 19:571–590. [17]

Miller, Philip H. 1991. *Clitics and Constituents in Phrase Structure Grammar.* Doctoral dissertation, Utrecht. Published by Garland, New York, 1992. [51]

Miller, Philip H., and Ivan A. Sag. 1997. French Clitic Movement Without Clitics or Movement. *Natural Language and Linguistic Theory* 15:573–639. [59–60]

Mohanan, Tara. 1988. Causativization in Malayalam. MS, Stanford University. [19]

Mohanan, Tara. 1995a. *Argument Structure in Hindi.* Stanford, CA: CSLI Publications. [21]

Mohanan, Tara. 1995b. Wordhood and Lexicality: Noun Incorporation in Hindi. *Natural Language and Linguistic Theory* 13:75–134. [21]

Monachesi, Paola. 1993. Restructuring verbs in Italian HPSG grammar. In *Papers from the 29th Regional Meeting of the Chicago Linguistics Society*, Vol. 1, 281–295. Chicago Linguistics Society. [60, 62]

Monachesi, Paola. 1995. *A grammar of Italian clitics.* Doctoral dissertation, Tilburg. ITK Dissertation Series 1995-3. [59–60]

Moore, John. 1990. Spanish Clause Reduction with Downstairs Cliticization. In *Grammatical Relations: A Cross-Theoretical Perspective*, ed. Katarzyna Dziwirek, Patrick Farrell, and Errapel Mejías-Bikandi. 319–333. Stanford, CA: Stanford Linguistics Association. [56]

Morrill, Glyn. 1994. *Type-Logical Grammar*. Dordrecht: Kluwer. [1]

Norwood, Susan. 1987. Grammátika del Sumo. MS, CIDCA. [92]

Pollard, Carl, and Ivan A. Sag. 1987. *Information-Based Syntax and Semantics*. Vol. 1. Stanford, CA: CSLI Publications. [55]

Pollard, Carl, and Ivan A. Sag. 1994. *Head-Driven Phrase-Structure Grammar*. CSLI Publications and Chicago University Press. [1, 7, 55, 60]

Rizzi, Luigi. 1978. A Restructuring Rule in Italian Syntax. In *Recent Transformational Studies in European Languages*, ed. Samuel Jay Keyser. 115–158. MIT Press. Republished as Chapter 1 in Rizzi (1982). [9, 26, 62–63, 83]

Rizzi, Luigi. 1982. *Issues in Italian Syntax*. Dordrecht: Foris. [27, 47, 53–54, 56–57, 66, 133]

Rosen, Carol. 1990. Italian Evidence for Multi-Predicate Clauses. In *Grammatical Relations: A Cross-Theoretical Perspective*, ed. Katarzyna Dziwirek, Patrick Farrell, and Errapel Mejías-Bikandi. 415–444. Stanford, CA: Stanford Linguistics Association. [59]

Rosen, Sara. 1989. *Argument-Strucure and Complex Predicates*. Doctoral dissertation, Brandeis University, Waltham MA. [45, 51, 59, 86]

Salamanca, Danilo. 1988. *Elementos de la Grammatical del Miskito*. Doctoral dissertation, MIT, Cambridge, MA. [90–93, 95, 97, 110]

Sebba, Mark. 1987. *The Syntax of Serial Verbs*. Benjamins. [103, 105–106]

Simpson, Jane H. 1983. *Aspects of Warlpiri morphology and syntax*. Doctoral dissertation, MIT. [5, 19, 22]

Simpson, Jane H. 1991. *Warlpiri Morpho-Syntax*. Dordrecht: Kluwer Academic. [16]

Wiklund, Anna-Lena. 1996. Pseudocoordination is Subordination. *Working Papers in Scandinavian Syntax* 58:29–54. [110]

Wilawan, Supriya. 1993. *A Reanalysis of So-Called Serial Verb Constructions in Thai, Khmer, Mandarin Chinese and Yoruba*. Doctoral dissertation, University of Hawai'i. [103, 105]

Wilson, Stephen. 1997. Coverbs and complex predicates in Wagiman. Honours thesis, University of Sydney. [19, 34–35, 37, 43]

Zubizarreta, Maria Luisa. 1985. The Relation between Morphophonology and Morphosyntax: The Case of Romance Causatives. *Linguistic Inquiry* 16:247–290. [59, 116]

Index